WHEN I WAS 7

special thanks

to the hundreds of you who participated in this project and shared a memory. To Diane Hansen (Mom) for helping separate the stories into categories. And to Bana Alabed for sharing her experience of the war in Syria with the world and spreading a message of peace.

———

Stories Curated by Phil Hansen
Cover design and internal illustrations by Katie Marek
Text layout by Tyler Zwirtz

D1568828

Phil in The Circle
PO Box 548
Chanhassen, MN 55317

Printed in the United States of America

First Edition

ISBN-10: 0692413081

philinthecircle.com

A note before you read-

This book has over 600 short stories from over 600 different people. These stories are unique moments in people's lives from the age of 7. The stories are not connected with each other; please read each story (section of text) as its own. Together they show a tapestry of what life can be at the age of 7.

Also, the stories people shared were sent in via text message. The decision has been made not to correct the messages in any way. You will see them as they are: spelling mistakes, capitalization goofs, missing punctuation, and some places where autocorrect changed things so much that it's hard to know what is happening. But that is part of the Ed toy mint.

CONTENTS

CONTENTS

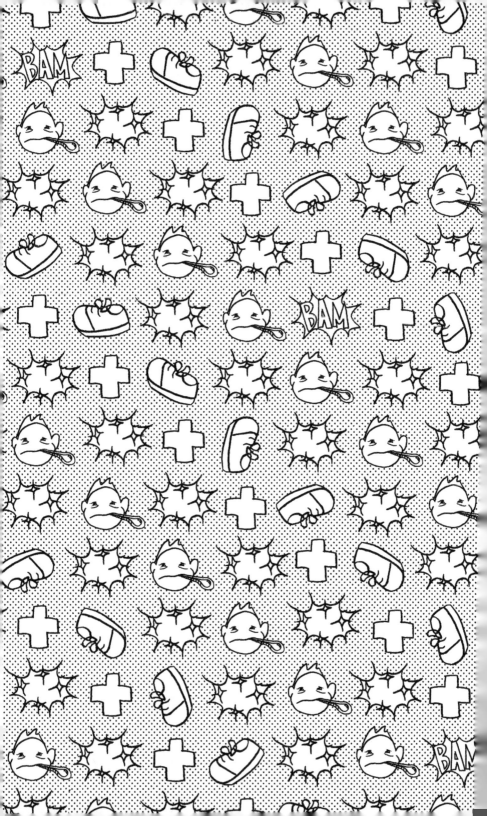

JUST WALK IT OFF

when i was 7 years old, i stepped on a nail that went through my foot. it was removed a week later by a doctor who inquired a rather large nurse to sit on my leg during the operation, restricting me from moving. no anesthetic was used, no numbing cream. he pulled it out with pliers. the screams could be heard from the waiting room.

i ran into a pitchfork at my grandparents. it went into my foot and almost broke the bone. it required stitches.

i remember walking off the counter in my kitchen becauae i thought i could walk on the air like indiana jones if i had enough faith. i fell on my face twice because i thought i could do better the second time.

i got a new bike and it had a passenger seat on the back. my friend drive and i ride down a steep hill. my heel got in the spokes and we crashed. i had to get stitches and use crutches which was a huge hit at recess!!

while playing tag i fell off a 2 story cliff onto my head

3

OUCH

when i was 7 years old my sister got a mountain bike for christmas. it was unseasonably warm that year so we went out and rode around our cul de sac. i slipped on a pile of sand and just laid there out of breath. without realizing what was to be my fate. my sister unfamiliar with the handbreaking system on her new hog started to pedal backwards, and to no avail did not slow her speed. the result; the nubby tire ran directly over my face and ripped the skin open from eyebrow to cheekbone. hanging pieces of flesh looked like crimson ribbon as i looked over my wound in a hand mirror before fleeing to the emergency room.

we went skiing in austria. i turned 7 while i was there. i took a big fall down the mountain and ended up staying in our hotel with everyone who worked there. i got to go in the kitchen and see all the rooms. then they made me a super special birthday cake. and it was gross. but it was so sweet that they did that for me!

i was at the park climbing up the slide ladder (back when they were 10 ft tall metal slides), when i got to the top, i fell off the side onto my face. i had gravel embedded in my forehead but didn't break any bones! i still have some light scars on my forehead from the accident, but they've faded a lot. i'm pretty sure that's why i have a fear of falling and heights

when i was 7, the year was *1985*, i got my first major sunburn. being a filipino/irish girl from san diego that was a hard task. my neighbor told my stepmomthat i had done something, and she wanted to talk to her about it. so, my stepmom asked me what i did. i wasn't about to give her anything (there were a few things i could've gotten in trouble for, and i didn't know which one she was going to find out about) so, i said nothing. she made me sit outside until i told her. 9 hours later!! i still said nothing!! needless to say--major sunburn. i don't remember what it was the neighbor had on me...

4

OUCH

when i was 7 my dad and i were in a really bad bicycle accident that resulted in both of us in the hospital with amnesia. what's crazy is how many clips of crystal clear memories i have leading up to the accident. i remember the clothes i was wearing and being excited all day at school about going to a friend's house in the afternoon. i remember questioning my dad when he put me on the bar of his bike and suggesting we walk the bike down the big hill between our house an my friend and then nothing. no one knows what happend, if my foot got stuck in the spokes and we rolled down the hill or if we were hit by a car. the next memory i had was waking up in the hospital with my best friend looking down at my face and loudly uttering, "eeeew."

when i was 7 years old... my parents were having a new roof put on the house. as i was walking into the front door, one of the roofers accidentally dropped a hammer. the pointed end hit me on the top of my head. i didn't realize it at first but then felt something running down my face. it was blood. my mom rushed me to the hospital. my head was stitched up and i was ok, but my mom was told that if the point had gone in 1 centimeter more, i may have had significant brain damage. thank god that was not the case!

i was playing hide and seek with my brother and friends in my dads farm in ocala and i tripped on a tree root, knocking my front 2 teeth out

my sister and i were playing witches
and wizards but we were fighting
over who got to use the bristle
broom to ride on. i had a firm hold of
the broom by the bristle end and my
sister had the handle. a tug of war
ensued and she got fed up and let
go of her end causing me to pull the
bristles into my right eye. i scratched
my cornea and had to wear an eye
patch for a month. we played pirates
after that for a while due to the
patch until we got into harry potter.

only time ever visiting nyc
and i got a splinter in the
bottom of my foot that was
almost the entire length of
my foot.

When I was seven years old, two
major things that shaped my life
happened. I had a bad accident that
has since been the cause of chronic
migraines that I can't shake or get the
right treatment for. And my mother
was diagnosed with ovarian cancer.
Sadly she lost her battle when I was
12, but her memory still shapes me
to be the fighter I am today against
everything that comes at me.

ouch

my nane is mike, when i was 7 my best friend and i were out riding our bikes. i stopped by a small bridge and walked on the concert sides. my friend jeff rode up next to me and put his foot out to rest on the concert. his foot slipped, knocking my legs out from me and i feel to the stream below. only 10 feet but my head hit   some rocks and started bleeding. luckily i was ok after going to the doctors but i still remember getting a tetanus shot which hurt worst!!

when i was seven i fell off my bike and twisted my ankle but i studied a lot more from it

i was in the playground at school when another kid kicked a ball in my face and i fell back onto the concrete. i was dizzy and staggered into the school office and my grandparents were called. i remember laying on the floor using my jacket as a pillow. i later found out i had a concussion.

i was on top of a slide at school and pushed by a boy behind me causing me to fall off the top of the slide hitting my head on the ground.

falling off my bike

back when i was 7, i use to play hide-n-go seek with my two neighbors aaron and douglas... one day while aaron was seeking douglas and i, we climbed over a pile of used construction lumber to get away... aaron followed us, fell on the pile, and as he stood up we noticed a small board with a nail stuck to his head! being only 7, we ran away! aaron was the kind of kid that liked the crust off a pop-tart the most... i guess you can say he turned out just fine lol

7

Ouch

when i was 7, my skirt got caught on a random nail in the train at a mcdonalds playground. when i jumped off, i fell and hit the gravel so hard my forehead split open. i was more concerned about my blood stained shirt and skirt than i was the gushing wound. as an adult i'm more concerned that my family didn't sue over what became a scar i have to look at everyday.

i fell from a tree swing over a brick street. i boy untied it from the trunk while i was in full up swing. the place on my head was so big you could hold it and move it like a water balloon. i missed a day at an amusement park 😩 🎡

I got my pinky finger slammed in an apartment front door. It hurt... BAD, and the tip was essentially hanging on by skin. So I got it repaired in the ER, and had one of my most memorable photos taken. With my hand all bandaged, showing my tough guy-ness... with my mullet haircut I had at the time!

When I was about 7, I was playing on a "Turtle" scooter (self-propelled, sitting riding toy) incorrectly. I was kneeling on it with one knee, and pushing with the other leg. Completely forgetting the inlaid drain pipe in the sidewalk, the front wheels went into it, I go flying forward, and my front two teeth got pushed back up into my gums. Fortunately, they were my baby teeth and eventually came out on their own. And that they didn't affect my adult teeth when they came in later.

When I was 7 I was on my way to the car to go to the park and fell down the stairs and cut my leg. I still have the scar ten years later.

i was riding my bike, fell and skinned my knees and elbows

when i was seven years old i fell over the stair railing in a two story building, crashing to the cement floor below onto my face. i didn't break anything and was luckily just bruised up.

ouch

BROKEN BONE

when i was 7 years old i fell off a cliff and broke leg while on a class field trip. it was the **80's** so nobody sued anyone! lol

when i was 7 i broke my nose diving into a pool that was too shallow at a party at my house

when i was 7, i was running and sliding on a wood floor at a superbowl party. i tripped over a gus foot and flew face first into a class coffee table breaking my nose, and bleeding all over the place!

breaking my nose while playing frisbee at my old yellow house.

OuCH

at age 7, the toboggan i
was riding in hit a hill at
an odd angle and we were
propelled in the air. i fell on
ice and the other two girls
fell on me, crushing my
right collar bone. i was in
a brace for 16 weeks. this
brace had to be adjusted
every week and this
process was painful. as a
right handed child, there
were limitations of writing,
eating, personal hygiene. i
learned to do these things
with my left hand. i became
ambidextrous, which is
incredibly beneficial in
many areas of my life.

when i was seven years
old i was climbing a tree
in my friends' backyard. it
wasn't very high but when
i reached up to grab a
branch, the small branch
broke under my weight. i
fell to the ground holding
the branch. when i looked
at my arm on the ground,
i noticed that it was in the
shape of an s-curve. i
screamed. i grabbed my
arm with the other hand
and apparently set my
wrist. when all the parents
heard me, my mom said,
"that's not my child. she
doesn't sound like that!"
none of them thought it
was broken but we went to
the hospital anyway. doctor
showed us the x-ray. i
broke both bones. i set it,
too.

ouch

my family and i watched in awe of the opening ceremony. the flying man with his jet propulsion backpack was just out of this world. needless to say the impact it had on my brother and i was tremendous. i remember that we waited for the commercial break ran outside and jumped off the roof of our house. my brother fell ok, but i broke my arm.

as a 7-year-old girl, i loved playing on the playground at recess. i would play on the monkey bars and swing from ring to ring on the ring set. in california we had phenomenal playgrounds back in the 60's. at home i liked to swing from the bar that held up the swings on our swing set so i could go high. the day before halloween, i flew off the top bar of our swing set and broke my arm. not only did it hurt, but i wasn't able to carve the jack o'lantern at school the next day. that was more painful than the break!

i broke my arm and it was about ten minutes before we left to go the emergency room and i ended up falling asleep on my broke arm

My sister, Pam, and I were counting the days until summer and already enjoying playing outside after dinner. One night she kicked a ball towards me and called, "Get it!" As I went to retrive the ball, she ran to beat me to the ball and threw me down to prevent me from grabbing the ball. I started crying and soon discovered my arm was in rough shape. A trip to the hospital confirmed a broken arm. The memory of that heavy plaster cast being worn all summer seems like yesterday. I could not swim or participate in most summer activities. I do remember extending a knitting needle inside the cast to scratch my itchy arm.

OUCH

When
I was
seven, I
was riding
a bike too
big for me, fell
flat on my face
on concrete and
broke nose. My oldest
sister, Jen, scooped me
up and ran home me with me.
By the time we got there, a short
distance away, my white shirt was
red with blood. My grandmother, who
was babysitting, lay me on the kitchen
floor and put ice on my nose. To this
day, I have a small scar on my nose
where it broke. To this day, Jen
is still taking care of me when
I fall on my face.

ILLNESS

when i was 7 years old i had to have a double hernia operation. i remember laying in the hospital bed and crying because the doctors were going to give me a shot and i was terrified of needles (still am!) i also remember that i was allowed to have one of my parents stay overnight with me at the hospital (the other parent had to be home with my siblings) and i picked my dad. still feel guilty i couldn't have them both with me. mom slept on the floor next to me while i recovered for the next week or so.

memories of me at 7 years old. i was sick. my mom put my ponytails up in socks. i was sick. my mom told me i could still go to school.

I remember being checked into the hospital for my 10th hip surgery. I was waiting with my mother and could hear the phlibotomist coming down the hallway to take my blood. As soon as I heard the clink clink clink of the test tubes in her cart...I became hysterical. My mother held me. It was surgery number 10 out of 22.

OUCH

i got both my tonsils and adenoids out the summer i turned seven. they had to wait till after i recovered from chicken pox to do the operation. it was the only time i've ever been in the hospital overnight. neither of my parents were able to stay with me. i sat up all night in a darkened hospital, drawing flying saucers and space monsters, following the step-by-step instructions in the book my mom had given me before heading home.

when i was 7 i had my first bleeding peptic ulcer. i was hospitalized for what seemed like months but was really a week. this illness sparked my interest to help others...and today i am a physician.

When I was 7, I had my tonsils removed. I remember being so scared to be put under general anesthesia because I was scared that I would never wake up. My mom had to hold my hand and the last thing I remember is a mask to give me laughing gas being put on and then drifting into nothingness. The only other thing I remember about the actual surgery was throwing up the orange popsicle they gave me. I missed school for a whole week and a half to recover, which for me was a travesty. But my teacher gave me a get well soon gift bag, and in it was a worm Beanie Baby because I was such a bookworm. I was so happy that my teacher cared so much about me, and gave me such a specific gift instead of something generic.

SENSES

i remember getting glasses
for the first time and seeing
the leaves on he trees. i
had no idea they looked
like that! my world changed
that day.

SENSES

following my grandfather like a shadow all around the farm. he knew the trees by the bark and every flower that covered the ground. how large he seemed - he was probably 6'3" but he seemed like a giant. he smelled like tobacco and the barn. if you grew up in the country you know what i mean. the barn has its own smell. safety. love.

i was in second grade when i was seven. the teacher, mrs. grinipn was a large woman who hated disruptions in class. she had a big piece of wood that she would slam on the desk whenever children were disruptive which was often. with every slap of the wood on the desk my body would freeze with intensity. i had violence and uncertainty in my home. i never knew when the yelling throwing things in the beatings would come.

i had an old polaroid camera with me that used to belong to my mom. i brought it to a playground where i met some kids, new friends i guess, and we took lots of goofy pictures in this big wooden playhouse in the playground. it smelled like wood chips, and there were lots of wasps, but i played with these strangers for a few hours, left, and beer saw them again. it's kind of neat having pictures of us now and not knowing who or where they are.

when i was 7, i got my first hearing aid and i could hear words for the first time. when i was 21, i got 2 hearing aids and i heard rain for the first time. when i was 26, i found out i was going blind so i became an occupational therapist. last year when a therapy company wouldn't hire me because of my disabilities, i opened a private practice.:)

When i was seven i used to go out to our back alley. It smelled like gasoline, and I loved that smell so I would go back and lick the dirt.

18

SENSES

i still remember the clear voice of french singer Dalida, that my aunt loved very much, in my aunt's chill living room, from her vinyl player. After all these years hearing Dalida's songs takes me back to when I was a kid, when everything was simple. No internet, no mobile phones. Her unique voice reminds me of a time when my father, grandparents and aunts were still alive.

Waking up to clickrty-clack of train flying down tracks. Foggy-headed until eyes raise to the window - sitting bolt upright as the massive L.A. Harvest Moon fills the window, Had no idea there were moons this large.

When I was seven, I started working in the tobacco fields with my family. I walked row after row in the hot Kentucky sun trailing my uncle's tractor. I can still taste the sweat, smell the wet soil, and hear my cousins laughing. Hard work married to laughter bears the brightest memories.

sometimes smells will bring back a memory. everytime i smell limes or diesel it reminds me of my grandmother. she lived in mexico and it was always an adventure visiting her. she had a lime tree in the back of the house were everyone gathered. she had such beautiful natural smelling fruits and flowers. even know there will be certain smells that bring my grandmother back to me.

i have a memory of one of the times my father came home upset from work... which would happen alot.... followed by drinking.... now being an adult myself is understandable....however these incidents would turn out to be the framework of my dysfunction..... having been told that i need to be prepared for the world and not to get my hopes up because the world would screw me over everytime it had the chance. i remember the tone...as well as the stench the scotch left in the sweat on his skin. i'm 54 and still trying to fix the negativity this left me with.

SENSES

on the eve of my 7th birthday my mom made
me a cake with my (still) favorite rainbow
chip frosting. the smell was overwhelming
and i couldn't sleep. after everyone went to
bed i got up to check it out. one finger swipe
turned i to two, then ten, and before i knew it
that cake was naked. i tossed and turned and
finally woke up my mom to apologize. i told
her i couldn't help myself and she laughed
like i've never heard her laugh since. she
said because i was honest and it was my
birthday, that was it. every few years she gets
me a jar of that frosting.

my father was perfect. but he was a
smoker. i didn't like that. smoking was
stinky. smoking could kill him. i wanted him
to live forever. one morning i put a note in
his attaché case: stop smoking!i figured he
would read that, and see reason. my father
was a salesman. when he came home from
work that day, he was not grateful to me
for saving his life. he yelled at me for his
embarrassment at his customers seeing
this message in his attaché case. but the
following week, he softened. he decided he
was going to quit smoking, cold turkey, and
use the funds he saved to take the family
to florida. he calculated how many packs
it would take, and made a big poster with
the word florida blocked out in rectangular
segments, each evoking the shape of a
cigarette pack, and representing a week
without smoking. with each successful
week, he would color in another segment. i
think he made it to f l

PARENTS

PARENTS

when i was 7, my parents took my sister and i to disney world. when we returned home they sat us on the couch and told us they were getting a divorce.

i leaned over the back of the couch, watching out the window as my dad walked down the sidewalk to his car. my mom was faintly crying in her bedroom. she wouldn't watch him leave, even though she made him do it. i had a sick feeling in my stomach, knowing something was different, but i didn't understand until later that he was leaving for good. that my life would never be the same.

In my 7th birthday, my parents took me to Chuckee Cheeses and made use a buttoned shirt and tie that I hated. But that day ended being one of my favorite childhood memories. So grateful for my family.

i once got lost in a huge water park for almost an hour before my parents found me luckily.

seeing my parents fist fight each other in my kitchen. :(

when i was 7 years old my mother married our new step-dad and he brought along 4 of his own kids to add to me and my sister and brother. his kids were older - two out of the house and two still in high school. these two boys in hs combined into our living space and the changes were both exciting and frightening. there were so many promises for good but the reality was messy and nightly highballs were introduced into our world. alcohol took its toll and the marriage ended by the time i was 16. the whole experience was ultimately devastating and i ended up running away from home and being estranged from my family until i divorced with my two daughters and needed help from my mom. wish it all could have been better than it was but i am now 59 years old and have made my peace with parents who have died decades ago.

PARENTS

it's quiet and dark. the star shaped stickers on my bedroom ceiling are begining to dim as the glow in the dark paint looses its charge. i lost my first tooth today and its tucked carefully under my pillow in a zip lock bag. i am too excited to fall asleep. does she have wings? does she reallt fly? then there is nothing. i wake up and where my tooth once was is a wrinkled dollar bill. she came!

i don't usually talk about my childhood because i have very few good memories. my father went to prison for the 1st time because he beat my mother up really bad.

my parents got divorced when i was 7 years old. my mom & i moved to roanoke va and left washington dc, and my daddy, behind us. i didn't see my daddy again until I was 9.

i don't have memory as a child. it's a fog and a mist. i've asked my family about memories. mom and dad remember a lot. my brother has missing memories too. in my search for my memories i have discovered that i've hidden and repressed the memories. i grew up in a household where neglect and emotional abuse stole my memories. i love my parents and credit them with me being who i am today. now i spend my days making sure i am creating amazing memories for my wife i love.

when i was 7 years old i was sitting on the grass with my mom and my dad came running out of the house screaming that he hates my mom and got a divorce with my mom, i thought for the longest time that it was my fault.

PARENTS

i remember
my parents
w   e   r   e
building   a
spare room
onto   our
trailer. they
said it was
b e c a u s e
they wanted
a n o t h e r
room for us
kids   since
the   three
of   us   were
sharing a small
room. i would go
in there to play with
my pokemon cards with
some   nieghborhood   kids
because it looked so cool with the
exposed wires. i found it funny one day
that the doorway was blocked off, so i crawled
through a hole they planed to put a window on.
inside i saw some strange amalgamation of tubes
and glass. my parents found me in there and were
livid. they said it was a top secret science experiment
they were working on and that we couldn't go in there
anymore. the room was never finished and many years
later i learned that my parents were making meth. i
believed my parents because i had such respect and
love for them, so that thought never crossed my mind.
my sisters knew, but never told me. i wish they would
have so i didn't feel so small and naive when i
learned the truth. even now though, i think i trust
too easily, so i avoid forming bonds with
others so i won't get hurt.

PARENTS

i heard my mom screening. i knew my parents were arguing, and my dad was probably hitting her. i ran in the room and stiff in horror add he had her by the hair and bashed her head into the corner of a piece of furniture. i ran over in between them. i used every ounce of energy i had to kick and push him away from her. her head was bleeding, i remember that well. he backed off. i pushed her into the kitchen to get a towel for her head. my little sister ran and sat in het lap. our dad wouldn't touch her if my sister was in the way. no one ever knew what happened. the next day at school was a hard one, but no different than other days that followed a fight. i always wished a teacher or someone would ask me what happened our how my night was so that i could say something... but they never did.

My mom divorced my dad because he was an alcoholic. He tried his best to get sober, but couldn't. I never saw my dad again.

when i was 7 years old, my parents divorced and i ironically thought it was amazing. i would get 2 houses, double the birthday presents, and special time with both parents individually. as my parents were divorcing, we were moving to florida from minnesota at the same time. everyone in my family now had awhole new life. two things, divorce and a big move, that most people would find tragic and sad and miserable, my family and i found the greatest happiness of our lives

when i was 7, my parents got divorced. they had separated before, but it was different this time. my mom sat me on the couch and told me daddy moved out and he wasn't coming back this time. we both cried for a very long time. i'm crying right now, actually.

when i was 7 my parents got divorced and we moved to another state, i read a lot of books that year to cope and most of my memories are imaginary ones from then

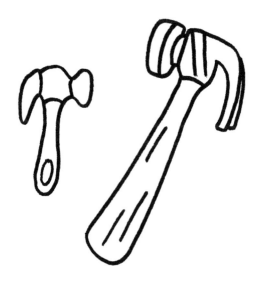

DAD

i went to new hampshire with just my dad for family work weekend which is when my grandparents turn over their house from winter to summer. it was the 1st time my dad & i went away without my mom & sister.

my dad was deployed oversees to afghanistan for a year

27

PARENTS

As we went home one day, Dad spotted a small grass fire in a vacant lot a few doors from our house. At home, Dad soaked a burlap bag and carried it to the vacant lot, so I went to see what he was doing. He started beating on the fire by swinging the wet bag over his head and smashing the fire and grass into the ground. That looked like fun, so I went home and wet a burlap bag for me to use in fighting the fire. I found out real quickly that swinging a heavy wet bag over my head and into the fire and ground was hot and hard work. I was good for about three swings before resting again.

when i was seven years old my father had an affair with a woman he worked with and it put my mother into a deep depression.at the time i was just a child and i didn't understand why mom packed all of his things. i didn't understand why daddy had to leave. later i understood her hurt when i soon found out that the other woman's children got to spend more time with my father than i did. i begin to understand my mothers pain i felt replaced and i know that's exactly how my mother felt only 100 times worse. i went from seeing my father daily to one hour visits a week if i was lucky. my mother overcame her depression and i soon realized that if my mother could live without him so could i.

PARENTS

when i was seven i had a bad infection in the bone of my foot and it was as painful to walk. we were on family vacation and my dad carried me piggyback everywhere so i wouldn't miss anything.

when i was seven years old i remember my dad being the leader for the girls scout troop after none of you other moms wanted the position. ♡

7 years, 2nd grade. why was i picked on so much. how did they not understand i would retaliate when they were my same age, same height same weight, that was fair compared to the nightmare waiting for me. they start it, i end it. sent to the office again. sent home early again. moms at work, dad picks me up. three block drive, seven minutes of silence. god i hate the silence. a few steps in the house. six times my age, double my height; three times my weight. six hits, two kicks &ends with three words. love you son

my father is an alcoholic when i was 7 i wrote him a contract that said if you never drink again i promise to never be bad and to always listen to you i promise i will work hard and never make you mad ...when i gave it to him he read it crumpled it up and said he was my patent and i can't tell him what he can or can't do ...that day is the clearest memory of being 7 i have

there was a day when my dad (who is very masculine and "manly") stopped what he was doing and played pretty pretty princess with me. my mom came home and laughed to hard when she saw my dad wearing plastic jewelry and little tiara. 😭 🥹.

when mowing the lawn, my dad mowed my name "alisha" into grass and then knocked on the window so i could see his handiwork.

PARENTS

when i was 7 my dad lost his job. during spring break he took us on a pretend vacation to paris france. he build an eiffel tower in the living room out of tinker toys, hung travel posters of france, made us french toast and french fries, talked in a french accent, took us to the museum to see master pieces, bought us berets and stripped shirts and had us paint our own master pieces listening to french music and mimed for us. i always wanted to go to paris but doubt the real one would come close to the pretend one my dad made for us in 1977.

i remember watching national geographic with my dad. it was four years before he left without a word.

I remember my dad asking what we had learned at school that day. I told him we learned about insects and he said, "What?! You learned about sex?"

when i was 7 years old, i remember my father taking me on walks in a red radio wagon when i was in a green body cast. i was not able to get around easily but those walks were great.

hugging my daddy

when i was 7, i lost my dad. he was never much part of my life, but i knew somewhat about him. my mother was my father as well, and i never really knew what i was missing, except the thought of what it would've been like to have a dad. his funeral was the first one i attended. this is my memory from when i was 7.

my dad used to have "meetings" and miss my dance recitals.

my dad was a parasailing captain on the beach (the big parachute you hang from being dragged behind a boat) and he would always take me on the weekends. fondest memories of my dad are always us at the beach on the boat.

31

PARENTS

bundling me in a blanket
and carrying me outside.
i sincerely thought i was
being taken to a hospital
but instead he took me
outside just to look at the
christmas lights he hung
on the house. i still felt sick
but that lifted my spirits.
thanks, dad.

when i was seven my
father took me to
disneyland in an attempt
to bond with me and just
get closer. at the end of
the trip, i begged him to
quit smoking so we can
continue to go on trips
together. since then he has
quit and has been living a
healthy life smoke free for
20 years.

PARENTS

My dad and I are both very introverted people, we know there is a ton love between us, we just have an uncomfortably awkward way of showing it. At 7 years old he was/is still my hero. My dad was the smartest, hardworking man at NASA. He often worked 3rd shift and I remember getting yelled at by my mom because I'd sneak out of bed to fall asleep at the top of the stairs, just waiting for him to come home and tuck me into bed. I remember him and I building stuffed animal cages, robots or musical instruments... all sorts of imaginary things from some stupid plastic rings he brought home from work. They were only scraps from packaging but they interlocked, we are both super creative and I still have fond memories of those days. I recall how oddly-proud I was of my dad when, everyone jealously asked who the handsome man was. You see, he got called to my school after my cat managed to follow me and ended up sitting in the cafeteria! "That's MY Dad!" Odd are the memories you do recall... My dad shaped me, encouraged me and is the hero still within my 49 year old child eyes.

PARENTS

i was almost 8 years old in **1945** when my father had a devastating stroke that left him paralyzed on one side, unable to talk and with stroke induced dementia. i remember being awakened by his screams in the early morning. the evening before he had called the doctor to ask what to do for horrible headache. the doctor told him to take aspirin and go to bed. an ambulance was called to take him to the hospital. as i walk to school that morning with my neighborhood friends, i was quite excited to tell them an ambulance to come to our house that morning. i felt like a real celebrity! i think it was several years later that i remembered my elation at that distinction and how child like my reasoning was.

i remember when my mom informed me that her and daddy love me so much, but that daddy was not my real daddy. i was so upset, she promised that when i was older we would find my real dad.

When I was 7: My older brother went to live with my father in Winnipeg while I stayed with my mother in Nova Scotia. This is my earliest memory of meeting my father, as we all met in a shopping mall in Ontario for the hand off. I thought if I misbehaved I'd be sent away too. He eventually came home 4 years later.

i remember being about 7 and visiting my biological father in southern california for the summer. i was being punished for something, so he had my step-mom running me through multiplication cards she made with pen and paper. i was getting good at them because i could see the answer on the back. he came home from work and started testing me, discovered i could see the answer on the back, and then tested me without the cards. i 'failed' miserably... and that was the first time i remember him beating me. i don't own a single wooden spoon and the cracking of a belt will send my into a panic attack 21 years later.

PARENTS

MOM

it was past my bedtime, around 1am. my mother woke me up, put a coat on me, grabbed a blanket, and carried me outside. it was snowing. this may not seem like a big deal to many people, but it was 1989 in jacksonville, fl and this was the only time in my life that i have seen snow. my mom passed away a few years ago and this is one of my favorite memories with her. i remember it so clearly.

when i was seven years old, i testified as a witness against the guy who beat my mom for two years.

when i was 7, i was taken away from my mother. i remember being at the police stration and the police physically pulling me off of her, and then riding in a cruiser to my new foster parent's home. this was as sad as it sounds, but thankfully by 4th grade i was back with her full time.

PARENTS

i was going to sing in a christmas program at school. i was scared and told my mom i didn't want to go. she got down on her knees, hugged me, and said, "you know that funny feeling you have in your stomach?". i nodded yes. she said, "you can turn that into energy to help you sing", which i did. what i didn't realize at the time was the power of that statement. i've used that wisdom my entire life to go through a hard time instead of avoiding it. "the only way out of a scary situation is through it, and you have the power within you to conquer it!

i sat holding my head in my hands, weeping, because my mom was being put into an ambulance by two men as she yelled and screamed because she didn't want to go to the mental hospital.

i had some great memories at seven, it was 1986 and i lived in a double of weber rd in clintonville. my mother had finished her engineering degree and we spent a lot of time together. one snowy day we went to the park at the end of our street. the snow went up to my knees as we climbed the hill to go sledding. it was my first sled i got for christmas, you know the original wood and steel sleds. we had the most fun in the park. we made snow angels. i always had fun with my mom. that day was also memorable because she lost her keys and all i can remember is walking back and forth down weber road from our house to the park searching. unfortunately i don't recall if the keys were ever found or if we had to wait for my dad to come home. but i will never forget making snow angels with my best friend and angel, virginia. i love you mom.

PARENTS

i remember my mom crying, banging her head against the wall saying she was so depressed. then we got in the car, drove to disneyland, and acted like a normal family.

I wrote a letter to my grandmother in WV that said, "Mommy is haveing a bodle of shampain on 25 of May. Wednesday! You have to call and STOOP HER"

PARENTS

my twin and i were taken away from my biological mother. after living in foster care for a couple months we were adopted.

when i was 7 years old i remember my mother telling me she didn't want me anymore...

PARENTS

my first day of school walking home with my new friends i just met that day. i took a different route than my mom told me because my new friends lived around my neighborhood and went a different way. i didn't waste time but went the different route. my house was open but empty so i went in and watch tv. i found out my mom had waited at the crosswalk to walk me home. she came running into the house and when she saw me on the floor watching tv, she ran and gave me a hug first than proceeded to yell at me for not goinf the way she told me.

When I was 7, my mom made me go to Science Camp. I cried about being forced. Later, I learned that she had to fight to get me, a low income kid who wasn't doing well in school, into the camp. I went and still have memories of it 36 years later. It shaped my life and helped me become someone.

i had just been reunited with my mother after living in foster care for a year. as a single mom of two, and as a starving musician and singer, she had no choice but to leave us in la until she could find work and establish a home base for u in texas. she loved us more than any art form and so made it her overriding purpose to first reunite us, and then flourish and prosper as a singer in the late *70s* making a vinyl record of her songs with the texas rock band shotgun, and later another music cd in the rock band vision.

one time, my mom and i were shopping and she was annoyed at me, because i was an annoying child. i had to go to the bathroom, but i didn't want to bother her. i thought i could hold it, but i ended up having an accident in the department store.

PARENTS

i used to religiously
watch wwf wrestling with
my mother every week.
she was always working
so it was one of the few
things we were able to
do together when she
was home.

MOVING

Moving

when i was seven, i had just moved back to the united states with my mother, my mother had a generous friend, although we were very poor, i was enrolled in a very elite private catholic school, the transition and language barrier made me the resilient, strong person i am today. we moved here because of the earthquake in mexico city of 1985.

when i was 7 years old i moved from quincy, il to kansas city, ks. my dad had been working in kansas city for nearly 18 months and commuting back home as often as he could. it's not a long story, but i will never forget the moment we were all packed up, my mom, sister and i, following my dad and brother in the u-haul, and we pulled away from our neighborhood, i stared out the window with tears down my cheek trying to be strong, this was the only town i'd known, and the only town my mom had known, where all her family was. driving away from that house on s 6th street is a moment i'll never forget.

i moved from a small town in kansas to a big city in minnesota where i met my best friend, we have now been friends for 20 years!

i moved with my family from england to america. i was put in a 3rd grade class and all anyone could say to me was "say something!". i now look back and realize i had loads of friends, because like the spice girls, i was a british girl.

MOVING

when i was 7 we moved from chicago to wisconsin. i was so sad to be leaving our house and all my friends, i kissed a spot on the wood floor of the bedroom i shared with my sister before we left. every time something bad happened (i got stung by a bee, i did bad on my spelling test, etc) i was convinced that it was because someone stepped on the spot i kissed. i begged my mom to let me go back and knock on our old door and see if the new owners would let me wash the spot.

when i was seven my family moved from the south side of chicago to south texas. i started second grade with no friends and learned that we were poor. during gym class i was always followed by a certain couple of girls that would make fun of how poor i was and my "poor" clothes. i had no idea until they informed me. they thought it was hilarious.

when i was seven, i lived in russia, and i remember looking at an encyclopedia and seeing the map of usa. at the moment i didn't know it was in america, and i wished i would live in the usa. that year i found out i was moving to florida. best day of my life.

My life was changed in 1974... I moved from Kansas City, Kansas to a farm outside of tiny town of Cummings, Kansas. What an amazing life... growing up in the country! I was lucky enough to raise my kids on a farm, also. Nothing better!!!

at seven we lived in germany. i had began to lose my baby teeth, had worries that the toothfairy wouldn't be able to find me with us moving all the time, along with being in another coumtry from the u.s.! mom had asured me extensivelly that the tooth fairy, like santa covered all countries on the planet. however, my tooth became lost/misplaced bfor time for bed. since the tooth fairy was #1 favorite for myself, this was serious, how was she going to collect my tooth. my mom had me write a letter to tooth fairy with an expllantion of events of lost tooth, this done letter was placed undr pillow where toth was suppose to be, morning comes, i ck under pillow and bam note is gone replcing it was two dollars.. in my eyes it was like wow! she was so totaly awesome, she read my letter, and knew it was truth!. from then on if i had (tooth) i woulld try my best to stay awake to geta gliimpse of the toothfairy. well it became the biggest dissappointment for i seen whom the tooth fairy truly was, have a wonderful rest of the day

i don't remember to much
but it is the time i moved
from florida to oklahoma
and the first move i
remember (dad was in
the navy) i remember
feeling very scared and
apprehensive of being in
a new school and making
new friends.

When I was seven years
old I was the best speller
in my second grade class.
And then we moved to the
Philippines. My teacher
Mrs. Elle hugged me and
said "I'm losing my best
speller."

when i was 7, my parents
moved us from new
england to miami. my
cousins thought we'd be
lolling on the beach all
day, sipping on tropical
drinks. that's not quite what
transpired.

i was forced to leave
my home because of a
family conflict that could
have been fatal. i went
from school to school and
never felt like i fit in. my
childhood was a struggle
for everyone involved.

MOVING

interesting that you choose the 7. my father was living in us, and his girlfriend came to visit me in haiti. she asked my aunt if i could spend the night with her. my aunt said yes the following day she took me to ny. i know it was the month of december because i remember the christmas lights. that journey changed my life forever, it also taught me how resilient a child is. more importantly i think from a character standpoint, whoever you are at 7 your main character is established. naturally as you grow there will be minor tweaks along the way. i survived this journey because i was a child who was loved growing up. for a long time the memories of me being younger than seven were suppressed in an effort to move forward.

following my mothers divorce from my stepfather moving in with my grandparents

my family lived in oregon when i was 7 but we were moving to alaska. while everyone else was busy packing the household items, my twin brother and i thought it would be a good idea to use sidewalk chalk to draw little pictures all around the siding of the house our parents rented. they paid for a new paint job.

my parents moved the family from brazil to sweden when i was 7. it was a major cultural change for me that has shaped me who i am today.

when i was 7 years old, i moved to the city. it was a lot different from the ghetto.

when i was 7 we were getting evicted from our apartment i remember carrying my mouse name trigger to our car and not knowing where we were going to go.

moving to a new home and making new friends.

47

MOVING

when i was 7 my mom married my stepfather and my life changed for worse. not all at once but eventually. short vers... last few weeks of running through corn fields of ohio. next stop skating through streets of la. big deff. life changed became a 12 yo runaway. made it through all that. living the life of an artist is sf.

being told we were moving from the only home i had known. away from all of our family in mo to a place called texas. dad was going to work for a space company called nasa. i was scared, but my parents somehow made everything okay. my sisters teased me about being a baby. i ended up loving tx, and 52 years later, am still here.

HOLIDAYS

HOLIDAYS

i turned 7 in 1999 so all through my 7th year do you know what i kept hearing about? the glorious future and the terrifying y2k. so the whole year i kept thinking that as soon as the clock struck midnight on december 31st one of two things would happen. either giant skyscrapers, flying cars, and robots would suddenly appear in our world as part of our great new millennium or everything bad that could happen would happen. planes would fall from the sky, computers would explode, bombs would fall. chaos. so as new year's eve finally arrived i was just a bit antsy. either something really good or really bad was about to happen. midnight approached. i shut my eyes. the clock struck. ayld lang syne played and... nothing happened. no bombs, no flying cars. just the same as the before. i learned then just to take the future as it comes. don't bank all your hopes and don't live in fear. 17 years later i still take things one day at a time.

when i was 7 years old on christmas eve, i busted my chin on the kitchen floor, and had to be rushed to the er the night. that lovely christmas santa visited me while getting stitches placed inside my chin. definitely a christmas i'll never forget

i was in ms. summer's 2nd grade class and she asked us to create a scratch art project for mother's day. i spent evenings and any free minute in class planning. i eventually came up with a butterfly plan. i always thought my mom was perfect and to me butterflies are by far the most perfect creature on earth!!!!

we went to israel for a month. my dad was there for work, so mom, brother, and i went. it was december, and i was amazed not to see christmas trees everywhere. instead there was a giant menorah in the shopping center. very different from texas!

HOLIDAYS

y2k was upon us. my parents spent the better part of a month making sure that everything would work after midnight. i didn't understand, i was under the impression that the world would end at midnight, and i insisted on staying up all night just to see. of course, nothing happened. i wanted to throw confetti to celebrate the world not ending, but my mother refused to let me. we did blow some noisemakers, and scare the living daylights out of the cats.

it was **1976**. bicentennial 4th of july eating red white and blue cupcakes sitting on the back of my uncle john's old wooden houseboat. fireworks going off all around us as he played his guitar.

the delight of finding several wrapped christmas presents hidden under the kitchen sink. the disappointment of finding out my parents were santa. (sent with balloons)

i had my tonsils removed christmas eve day, and spent my winter break miserable, but full of ice cream and popsicles.

when i was 7, it was **1999**. i remember new year's coming and everyone freaking out. it was explained to 7 year old me that clocks wouldn't understand a new millennium, thus nuclear rockets would be fired off so a guy dyed himself blue to protect himself. nowadays that sounds like watch a neon blue man group concert stoned. but back then it was just nonsense. like, clocks were designed to keep going up. just the number two would be first. in retrospect, that is probably the first time i was truly a millennial. laughing about older generations freaking out about technology.

i dressed up as marie curie for halloween

i live on the south side chicago. there is a large population of irish (and decendents). on st. patrick's day, when i was 7, i went all out. i had a long twirly skirt with shamrocks, dee-diddle-boppers and green shirt. my teacher asked me and another student (who was from ireland) to be leprechauns. i got to spin around my classroom with my skirt leaving candy for my other classmates. i really felt like a leprechaun

christmas morning - on our piano bench next to the christmas tree, my dad set up a battalion of toy revolutionary war soldiers. blue coats and red coats facing off against each other. it was a wonderful morning of playing "army" with dad. it was the last christmas my parents would be married to each other.

i happen to be a 7 year old little girl at the turn of the century when it was new year's eve in *1999* wearing my 2000 glasses with the two middle zeros as the lenses watching the fireworks in downtown northampton massachusetts in the middle of the street with my parents in the freezing cold.

i was crying on the front porch worries that the easter bunny wouldn't know i was at my grandma's. my grandma came it and told me she had spoken to the easter bunny and he knew where to find me. the next morning i had a wind up pink bunny on the front porch that played music. i still have this pink wind up musical bunny a memory from 7 years old was so long ago i am 33 now, one memory i can remember was christmas that year we didn't have much, dad worked at pizza hut and land before time had just came out so they did a promotion. so for christmas he got me and my four siblings the dinosaurs from the movie and told us why he picked the ones he gave us. there was little foot (me) i was the curious one, spike(my older brother) he was the hungry protector, cera (older sister)sweet but strong-willed, petrie (oldest sister) the gentle kind hearted one, duckie (little sister) the silly one. he couldn't have been more right.

at 7, i was the oldest of four kids, living abroad. at christmas, there were no trees to decorate, so my mom pinned plain butcher paper to the living room wall and partitioned it so that we four kids could each decorate a section of the tree. it came alive and gorgeous with the drawings of four little kids and two parents who creatively kept christmas beautiful and full of wonder.

BIRTHDAY

i had a big birthday party. we had family and friends over all day. i spun on the yard swing and threw up afterwards because i was so dizzy. it was a great day.

i got a snoopy watch for my birthday

female friends 8th birthday, tripped a robber for a cop that was chasing him.

my 7th birthday party. all my friends from church, giant pixie sticks, new banana-seat bike! best time ever! june 1986.

HOLIDAYS

i started at a new school, moved to another part of town. with new friends. i had a surprise slumber party for my birthday and my parents had just pickedme up from a friends bday party only to stop to get gas and go to the store so that same friend could leave her house and get to mine before i showed up . it was a great surprise to join old and best friends from my old neighborhood with new ones in a surprise celebration all for me. made me feel more included and valued

At the time, we lived in a small German village due to my father's job in the U.S. Air Force. My mother told me I could invite whomever I wanted to come to my birthday party. Little did she know that I wanted to invite the whole village. After spending the majority of a day going up and down the streets inviting neighbor after neighbor, I returned home quite tired. My mother asked me whom I had invited, and I said, "Everyone!"

When I was SEVEN years old I was on top of the world it was my golden birthday October 7th 1967, I wish I was SEVEN years old all over again, I had no hatred, I had no prejudice and I loved everyone. I have changed and I'm trying to change back to how I thought about things when I was SEVEN.

HOLIDAYS

going to six gun territory
for my birthday. i was sure
i wanted to be a cowboy
when i grew up.

i remember sharing my birthday with my mother's best friend, the year i turned 7 and received this hat that made me look like blossom.
I felt like a total badass.

my parents forgot my seventh birthday. it fell on the same day as the super bowl that year and my parents had planned a big party for the game. i was an it was my birthday. i had been hiding in my room sulking all day, and was completly aware that i was ignored the whole day. 27 years later and it still hurts me that they both just forgot due to more important things. i haven't watched a super bowl game since.

the first birthday i remember was my 7 th. apollo 13 had launched on my birthday! everyone was so excited then became very worried for the astronauts return . my day went from an exciting landmark day feeling lucky to fear and worry for the next few days. i kind of thought i cursed it? like most 7 yr olds i was pretty sure the universe revolved around me ;)

i went to a red sox game on my birthday.

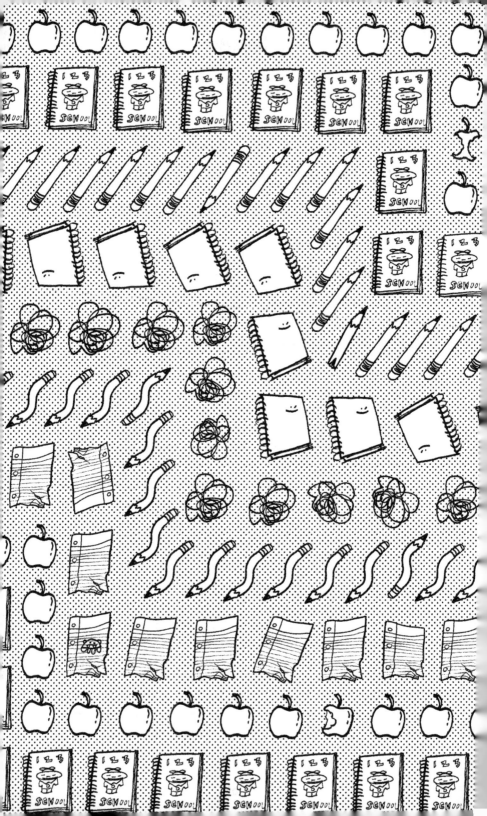

SCHOOL

playing kiss chase at school and with the neighbor kids. only got caught once. 😵

i was gretel in a production of hanzel and gretel by miss callahan, my 2nd grade teacher, in the one elementary school in whitinsville, ma.

in second grade i realized i didn't like math. at all. every assignment that was given, every homework sheet was stuffed inside my cubby below my desk. i didnt think this through at seven years old, because i remember my teacher had someone pull out all my stuff from my desk cubby where she found all the blank assignments. she ended up stapling them all together, called my parents and sent me home with a stack of math assignments i had to complete. i'm 43 and still hate math.

when i was seven i memorized the poem snowball by shel silverstein, and recited it to my class.

i was old for my first grade class and was way too rambunctious. during the next summer, my mom made me go to summer school and start swim lessons (both of which i hated with a passion. it was summer.....). when i showed up to school the next year, they ushered me to the third grade classroom, i then learned that my mom had skipped me a grade and i was terrified. bounced back as most children do, but it was a definite shocker which i remember vividly.

i had to repeat firat grade. i was sad because all of my friends moved on and i didn't. i felt like i was less than because i was held back

when i was seven and learning my multiplication tables, i could never do my practice sheet in under five minutes but there were two girls that could do it under one minute. i was always so impressed! years later, i found out one c heated the whole time. c'est la vie!

SCHOOL

when i was 7 i lived in russia in very rich community right next to my school. i had the best phone and cloths in entire school and i was pretty popular (unlike now). i had best friend named kate. we were together all the time. one day when we went to pe we all had to seat down and wait for our teacher to come and tell us what to do. my friend was a bit late so i asked a girl seating next to me named nastya to move so kate could seat there. on what she answered "you are a spoiled chicken!!" and run away in tears. every one was so confused and started laughing. including me. next class that we had was art.art has been always my favorite subject so teacher that we had loved me and considered me as her favorite student, but after that day she hated me with burning passion. as soon as everyone seat down at their seats, nastya came up to mine with kate's desk, took my pencil, broke it half, threw it at me and said "you are cursed now!", and sobbing went back to her table. me and kate were laughing so hard that everybody started too. teacher came up to crying nastya and asked her what's wrong. i don't know what she told her but, i remember that after their talk my teacher gave me this look and was ignoring me until i moved.

SCHOOL

when i was 7 years old
in 2nd grade we put on
a talent show and my
teacher asked who wanted
to participate. i raised my
hand without knowing what
we planned to do. me and
4 others volunteered and
my teacher told us we were
going to do the ymca song
by the village people. i
was the cowboy. it was my
first and last time being in
a talent show. i was quite
embarassed once i got up
on stage and i could hardly
hold it together while
singing, i was just laughing
the entire time. needless
to say i know all the lyrics
and motions to the "ymca"
and i even became a camp
counselor for the ymca
organization, which i did for
6 years.

i was in 2nd grade, we
were learning about johnny
appleseed and we watched
the movie with martin short
as johnny, and then we
made our own applesauce
right in class. i'll never
forget that.

when i was 7 my class
made salt dough santa
ornaments at school. i still
have him.

when i was 7 years old
my family lived in an
apartment outside of paris
where my father was a us
navy intelligence officer.
the whole year of second
grade i spent more time
traveling around europe
than attending school. this
would never be allowed
now but my schoolwork
was to journal and to draw
pictures of the places i
saw and the things i did. i
took that responsibility very
seriously. my report card
literally marked with more
absent days than present
days, but i passed to the
third grade!

this was in the **70's**. it
was show and tell at my
catholic school. i brought in
a record and played it, and
taught the class to do "the
hustle". seeing my teacher,
a nun in her habit sitting at
her desk, i said "come on,
sister, i'll teach you too."...
and she did. do the hustle!

SCHOOL

there was a girl in my class who wore the same dress every day. i didn't know it was the only one she had. one day some boys noticed she wasn't wearing underwear and they chased her around the playground, trying to pull up her dress. she fell and started to cry. the teacher ignored her pleas for help. several of us went to help her up and told the boys to leave her alone. still, the teacher just stared and did nothing. it was my first memory of feeling hate toward someone who wouldn't help a poor little girl.

i was 7, i was going on 35. one of my 2nd grade classmates, kevin, wad called "frosted flakes" by others in the class because he had dry scalp. they would run circles around him on the playground, yelling this name and i was certain he knew why. it broke my heart to see a kid be bullied even then. for a few days i agonized whether i should say something. i finally went to the teacher about it and the students got in trouble with the principal. instead of embarrassment, i felt proud of my decision. this is my earliest memory of my soft heart driving action in my life.

when i was 7: my entire 1st grade class learned all the words to 'what a wonderful world' by louis armstrong and we sang it to our pricipal when she retired later that year.

when i was seven, i remember practicing a bomb drill at school where we had to hide under our desks. i never wanted to leave school because i thought it was the only place i would be safe after that.

a memory i had when i was seven was when i skipped kindergarten. for me it really put into perspective my intelligence. that memory really means a lot to me.

I tested into a gifted program at school. I moved the next year and never got to experience it.

starting in a new school with no friends

i was in 1st grade when i was 7. i don't really have any memories of then :(

seven, i was in 2nd grade and i remember practicing writing my name in cursive.

in first grade, i used to always strive to be on the daily "phenomenal" list to make my teacher happy. there were many days when i wouldn't earn the spot to be on the list, and on those days i'd be so upset, because i tried so hard to be good. but on the days when i was on the list, i was full on life and felt on top of the world! i wonder if that phenomenal list sparked a desire to be the best, i.e., a perfectionist. oh how that desire to be the best has carried on throughout my life.

when i was 7 years old i remember being at school and a boy named andrew flipped out and started throwing chairs and knocking over tables. i don't know why he was so angry but this incident shocked me to the core. i had no idea that people could get so out of control.

SCHOOL

i remember a boy in my
second grade class,
alejandro, swallowed an
ice cube and was terrified
he would die, so the
teacher sent him out into
the courtyard to stand with
his mouth open wide facing
the sky, so the sunlight
would melt the ice cube.
never mind he was able
to breathe and talk the
whole time, and was in a
absolutely no danger. not
sure why i was sent out
with him, but i have a vivid
memory of standing there
holding his hand, watching
him stare at the sky with
his mouth open.

TEACHER

my second grade teacher's name mrs. tweedell, which always made me think of tweety bird. perhaps this was fitting, because every morning she used to make us stand by our desks and sing songs before she started teaching lessons for the day. she was old. and cute. but not so sweet. (shhhh, don't tell anyone i said that.)

that was the year my 1st grade teacher died from an aneurysm in the middle of the school year. the school brought my class outside to mourn. having no real concept of death, all the students played on the jungle gym and talked about dead pets. that was the last year that school was open. from then on, i was bused to a school in another town.

SCHOOL

when i was 7, a bunch of kids in my class decided to plan a surprise party for our teacher. we stayed in during recess and decorated her classroom. one of our parents brought an ice cream cake. we were all so excited. she noticed that we weren't at recess and came in to look for us. even after finding out that we were planning a surprise party for her, and that we were supervised (a parent was there), she proceeded to yell at us for breaking the rules and skipping recess. it kinda ruined the whole thing for us.

i had a teacher that would always get mad at the class and walk out for 10-20 minutes. it would always scare he class, but would always happen again.

SCHOOL

when i was 7 i won a pair of earrings at an arcade game. i didn't know who to give them to so i gave them to the teachers ade in class, and i also apologized to my teacher because i didn't give anything to her.

mrs. koston had just gone over the differences between fact and opinion in class. me, thinking myself a clever and charming second grader, sat next to her at recess to tell her, "you are the best teacher in the world, and that's a fact." she corrected me; it was definitely an opinion. despite my efforts to explain that i was in fact a clever and charming second grader who understood this, she assumed i just didn't get it.

my class did "really rosie" for the class musical and i was assigned to play johnny in "one was johnny." as a 7-year-old girl this was pretty upsetting to me at first so i went off to have a cry in the bathroom after being told how i was cast. i guess my teacher was aware enough to realize why i was upset and told me we'd change the part to janie instead. i guess this solution was enough for me because i did the play and still like the soundtrack to this day.

when i was 7, a substitute teacher tried to tell me my name was spelled incorrectly. it wasn't.

i had a second grade teacher that i loved ... mrs. klamfoth ... she sang ka ka katie to me!

when i was 7, i had the most beautiful teacher. her name was ms. finland. she wore purple eye shadow everyday she was also so kind. i wanted to be just like her when i grew up. purple is my favorite color to this day.

SCHOOL

it was 1978 in queens, n.y. just started a new school after a treacherous year in 1st grade at a catholic school where they tried to break my spirit with capital punishment, continuing to tell me i have no self control and a heavy dose of religion guilt. mrs. kramer was the first teacher who took my strong will spirit and made me soar. she respected my critical thinking and leadership skills that is a god given talent, and empowered me in a time and place within my journey that was filled with neglect, uncertainities and pain. i am now 45 years old and i will always be grateful for her!

when i was 7 years old, i remember being in my 2nd grade classroom. i was sitting at a table with my teacher practicing reading. she showed me where i had read over 100 books. i was very proud to have met that goal.

when i was 7, i loved my first grade teacher. i thought she was the kind of teacher i wanted to grow up to be. i was devastated to learn that she committed suicide last year.

i loved to climb up the jungle gym, but was too tall for the tube slide. one of the assistant teachers would pick me up everytime and bring me back to earth, only for me to climb up again. she never complained though, as i can remember.

i had a teacher explain why saying 'huh' as a response to a question was rude. she made the class reply in complete sentences. she was turning us into future respectful adults.

when i was seven, i was in second grade. my teacher was mrs leniart, my favorite so far. that year was my first communion (i'm catholic). i also had a lunch with my two favorite teachers that year. they were mrs leniart and mrs calabro, my music teacher. i got a very nice box from them that had a mini virgin mary in it. i was so happy and it was a great year. the sad part was that my dog died that year. her name was red and she was a samolian. i loved her to death and was devastated when she died the first week of second grade.

i was running outside at recess and looked back for a friend when i ran smack into a very "round" teacher and kind of bounced off her to the ground. took a while to live that one down!

my second grade teacher, mrs. sedney, told me i was so smart that i would get to use the 3rd grade reading book for the year. it was titled "serendipity". felt so proud and have loved the word ever since.

In first grade I had a teacher, Mrs. Kelly. Every day she would send a student to her mailbox. When it was my turn, I was super excited because I felt like this was a high class job. I proudly walked downstairs and out onto the street and realized I wasn't sure which house was hers, though I knew she lived across the street. I went back and told of my defeat and then she informed me I was supposed to go to the mailbox in the office, not at her house. I wasn't always a bright child.

in school my friend was swinging from an unsturdy pole and i ran to tell the teacher because we weren't supposed to, because it was unsafe. the teacher's only response was that i shouldn't be a tattle-tale.

SCHOOL

when i was 7 years old, i was in the second grade. i remember being pulled to work with a special teacher on reading. i had always been in high reading groups. this special teacher was working with the high readers on writing their own stories and carrying out the writing process. i wrote a story about a tiny little girl. i'd just read about thumblina and was interested in the idea of a small world like that. that special teacher gave me a bad grade and said it was because my story was not realistic. i don't remember being instructed to write a realistic story. she really hurt my feelings and made me feel like my imagination was stupid. i also remember my seventh year being the year i saw star wars for the first time.

when i was 7 me and my older siblings had been abandoned by each of our divorced parents so my father's girlfriend called his sisters to come get us before the state took us. we stayed a few days each with 4 different sisters families until they decided who would keep us. i spent the rest of the school year daydreaming staring out the window. the teacher yelled at me all the time. the next year my teacher was an artist! she brought in paintings she had done and played the violin for us! she recognized i loved art and was kind to me. it saved me. it was everything.

SCHOOL

even though my first grade teacher was strict and scary at times, i will always remember her fondly. we were talking about american presidents and a male classmate, vincent, asked if only boys were allowed to be president since he had noticed that all the past presidents were men. ms. delasandro responded by telling him no, that's not a rule and that she'd much rather have adrienne (me) be president than him.

i will always remember my favorite teacher 1968-69 second grade mrs cowart. she left a lifetime impression on me. she was so strict we had to use a brush to clean our shoes before entering her classroom. she was a very proper lady!

SCHOOL

Once when I was seven, I got shot down by the teacher
in front of the class. Not literally speaking ofcourse, but
they didn't like the fact that I knew things they didn't at
my age. I was having biology class and they wanted
us to talk about animals that were either odd or extinct.
And so I opted to talk about the Dodo. Unfortunately for
me the teacher kept insisting that such a thing never
existed. Note that the internet didn't exist at the time,
so we couldn't just look up the info over the web as you
can nowdays. So they resorted to look through a couple
of books that were present. I knew that the teacher had
one of the books with the info, since I had the same one
at home. I told her, and she looked in the book. She flat
out lied and said I was wrong, insisting I was talking
out of my ass. They were flat out lying in front of me
since I knew I gave them the right book and page. She
humiliated me for no reason and I never have been able
to completely forget that. I suppose it made me more
aware of what I talk about, and not trusting some adults.
I still can't believe that an adult teacher could do that to a
kid.

SCHOOL

when i was in first grade, my teacher brought pet mice into our classroom. i was extremely disappointed when she named the mice after the other children, butnot after me. one of the children stuck out in my mind the most, as in my child's mind i thought he deserved it the least. he would eat glue and wasn't as smart as i. he would regale us with tales of sleeping in a dresser drawer, and was often unclean. i could barely contain my hurt feelings in class that day, and cried on the bus ride home. as an adult, i look back and see the beauty in what my teacher did at the time. she made that boy beam with pride when he was one of the select few to have a namesake mouse. she made him feel special and important. we may not see the reason for things in the moment, but in time, if we are lucky, we see the bigger picture. now i'm a teacher. i truly love my profession, and i especially love my students. one of my favorite quotes is "a child needs your love the most, when he deserves it the least" by emma bombeck. may we remember great teachers, may we know great teachers, and may we all be great teachers.

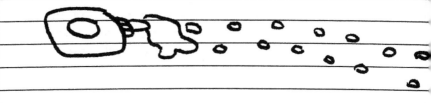

TROUBLEMAKERS

i got my first bladder infection at 7. i realized i could tell my mom it hurt when i peed and there was no way she could tell i was lying. i literally missed 87 days of school and had my bladder scoped because i wouldn't admit i was lying because i hated my teacher mrs juber that much. i always wanted to go back and tell her how much i hated how she treated me.

There was this boy in my class who would throw pencils under the girls desks to look up their skirts. My mom forced me to wear a dress to picture day. I was so anxious all day I hadn't eaten. By the time he threw his pencil under my desk, I was angry. I just stepped down on that boys face as hard as I could. I was sent home early and punished. But even then I knew I would do the same thing again.

SCHOOL

i was sent to the principal's office for asking a friend to lift up a female second grader's skirt.

i tried to be a power ranger by kicking this guy that was being a bully to one of my friends in school. keep in mind that he was a lot bigger than my short, skinny little-girl self, but go go power rangers straight to the stomach! it left a red shoe print on his torso. i left without my loose front tooth, due to him pushing me to the ground. top it all off, picture day was the next morning. my mom hated the pictures, but i hated not getting to watch power rangers for a week!

i turned 7 at the end of 1st grade. a little girl named tina bit me on the shoulder because i was too shy to talk to her. when i was 7, i hated subtraction so i changed all minuses to pluses. i was a problem solver!

in first grade i got in trouble for jumping over a bin of lunch boxes in the cafeteria at school.

i have a memory of the first time i was in trouble at school- i locked the bathroom stall and crawled out the bottom, not to be funny or cause any issues, but purely cause two other girls were doing it. i only did it once, and when my teacher found out she wrote my name on the board- which at that point was the most trouble i'd ever been in. i remember being so ashamed of myself for doing something even at the time i thought was pretty stupid

during school, a classmate told me he loved me and wanted to marry me. i casually stopped cutting my arts and crafts to grab a chunk of his hair and cut it off. that showed him how i felt about his plan. this is the only story i can remember to tell from when i was 7.

SCHOOL

when i was seven i was in 2nd grade in a catholic school in nj. it was an old building with big old metal radiators in the rooms. during recess me and a couple of friends snuck into an empty room and put crayola crayons on the top of the radiator and watched them melt and drip onto the floor. we got caught and had to scrape up the mess, but i still remember how cool the drips on the floor were - they ended up as swirly pools of mixed colors. i loved mixing colors with crayons and colored pencils on paper, like orange, red and yellow to make flames, etc., but this was on a different level.

i remember concocting bogus accusations about a first grade classmate i didn't like, and reporting them to our teacher. the dumb part is, the classmate actually admitted to the accusations and was punished for something he didn't do.

i was 7 when we moved from ny to fl. on the first day of school, i lied about my name. it wasn't until two weeks later that my teacher reached out to my parents and the record was set straight.

in class, i peed on my pants on purpose to get the class' attention.

For art projects we would wander over to another classroom, one day as we were picking up and about to go back to our classroom I thought it would be funny to rub a glue stick all over the seat I was sitting in for the kid who would come back to it would sit down unnoticed and as they stood up the chair would be stuck to their behind! No one would know it was me. Turned out the chair was so obviously covered in glue that the kid told the teacher and the teacher found me, grabbed me by the arm, dragged me back to the classroom, in tears, I had to clean up the chair in front of the entire classroom.

when i was 7 at recess i collected caterpillars from a tree and then let them free during story time in the classroom

when i was 7, i lied to my first grade teacher and told her i had a cat named princess. i was caught in this lie in the parent-teacher conference!

I have always been a fierce girl, since the kindergarten mother would have been called quite often by the educators because of the blunders I was doing and that would not change too quickly. In the first year of school when I was 7 years old I remember playing more aggressively whit my desk colleague and I broke a window from a door. Funny was not just the fact that we broke the window together, but the fact that my colleague's head went through the window. Fortunately no one was injured (at least that's what I remember) and the window? well the glass had to be changed, and since I was the one responsible, I called my grandfather to put a new window. this was a memorable experience and probably because not only my mother had to be called to school because of me, even my grandfather. Of course I was punished at home, but that didn't stop me from doing other very inventive blunders.

ACCIDENTS

i pee'd my pants at my desk because i wasn't allowed to go to the bathroom.

elementary school. swinging on monkey bars after it had rained all night. teacher comes over and tickles my underarms. fall into large mud puddle under monkey bars. muddy all day.

when i was in 2nd grade i had to go to the bathroom really bad but wasn't allowed to leave class. i peed my pants sitting at my desk in the middle of class. the only thing they had for me to change into was a costume from the school play so i had to wear the ridiculous outfit the rest of the day.

when i was 7 i was in 2nd grade and i was out at recess with my best friend jackie who is no longer alive today, and she made me laugh about something so funny that i peed my pants. i was beyond mortified and had no way to hide it so i was forced to make the long tragic walk across the playground to tell my teacher that i had peed my pants. i don't think i have ever felt that level of shame again. i can still feel the stiff cold wet feeling of my teal cargo pants as i walked, and the feeling of every student staring, laughing and pointing at my dark wet pee spot.

my classmate puked on my courderoy pants

when i was seven i was in first grade. we were having story time on the circle rug. i had to sneeze and farted at the same time. the kids all laughed and the one behind me moved, it was so embarrassing. i still think about it anytime i have to sneeze in public and i'm 30.

SCHOOL

i don't know why

i remember the bad, but it was a school day morning...i was up on the blackboard solving a problem i think... then i threw up my breakfast. not sure if it was nerves or indigestion but i could never forget 😖

in second grade i remember my class put on a play for tiki tiki tembo and i was able to be sam his brother even though i was a girl. looking back at it now i think some of the parents were a little weirded out by it but it was a blast singing and i felt so comfortable in that role. the other boy who was chosen was so nervous about performing he threw up at the end. but that instant sparked my love for singing, plays, and musicals.

i was in school and not feeling well, so i asked my teacher if i could go to the restroom. she said no. i proceeded to throw up in front of her desk and two more times on my way out of the classroom.

SCHOOL

My first participation in anarchy occurred when I was seven.
We were walking down the hall to a school wide assembly
in the gymnasium. The hallway was very slippery from the
invasion of the outside the children brought to school on a
slushy first snow of the winter in Alaska. Our teacher was
wearing high heels, they looked the ilk that my Grandmother
would wear, two point five inches tall. When she fell it was
almost comical, as a class we instinctively backed away. I
don't remember who exactly said it, but my memory is that
of a young boy saying we were on our way to recess and
should go out to the play ground. We all just ran away from
our teacher, who called out for help. I think a few students
actually stayed behind, but the rest of us had detention
in the library for what seemed like eternity. Our teacher
never wore high heels again, she broke her leg. My father
lectured me on mob mentality, for me it felt like the first time
I was free to do whatever I wanted. Reality gave me the
first glimpse of the illusion of freedom.

SIBLINGS

BROTHER

when i was 7, my mom was pregnant. i prayed every night that i would have a sister. when i found out that i was going to have a brother, i cried for hours. i was inconsolable. i thought if i kept praying for a sister that he would come out and be a girl. that didn't work either.

holding my newborn baby brother sean on my fathers recliner.

when i was 7 years old, my little brother was born with down syndrome. it meant much more responsibility for me as a kid, but it also meant a lot of memories filled with laughter and joy.

SIBLINGS

one time when i was 7
i was playing a game
with my brother and we
were laughing so hard
he pooped his pants.
it was hilarious

SIBLINGS

when i was 7, my 9 year old brother became a master at distracting me from our parents' constant fighting. they never seemed to notice when we would leave the house and spend hours collecting dropped change to spend at the penny candy store. when we were lucky enough to find quarters, they went in the bouncy ball vending machine. it happened often enough that we perfected the trick of the slow turn that gets two balls to drop instead of one

natural redhead oldest of three and the only girl. when i was seven i beat a third-grade boy up who hit my brother on the school bus. i took my red alf lunchbox and kept hitting him in the head until the bus driver pulled me off.

going to disney land and seeing tinker bell every night and my older brother had to take me. and of course he had an attitude about it. but i believe he in joyed taking me. this is a fond memory because my older and only sibling passed a way with cancer in his mid thirties

my brother attached a wagon to the back of a bike. it was the time of my life, until we were going around a cul-de-sac and i fell into a bush. i was laughing so hard until i came inside and i was covered in bruises. i immediately started crying because when i saw the blood i started to panic. my other brother had just taken his clothes out of the dryer and had placed it on top of me. it felt so good.

SIBLINGS

when i was 7 years old, the first of my love was born, my younger brother. he was my baby and i had prayed for a little buddy to play with. i was the happiest 7 year old alive!

When I was 7 my little brother Jay was born. Now I'm 64 and he is gone. He was killed in an accident on his motorcycle back in 2003. It happened on 9/10/2003, the day before the 9/11 2nd anniversary. Our family now has it's 9/10 just like our country has it's 9/11. We mourn and we celebrate the lives affected by his passing. You love me, Jay!

holding my baby brother after holding 3 sisters

my youngest brother was born 5 weeks prematurely. i wondered if he would still have "all those wires" on him when he came home. spoiler alert: he didn't

at 7 years old my mother was pregnant with my youngest brother joseph and i was very jealous of his arrival not knowing i would later lend a hand to help raise him...

as the youngest of six children, i remember writing letters to service men who were serving during the vietnam war. my brothers and sisters knew many who served and we often sent them encouragement.

SIBLINGS

SISTER

when i was seven years old i calmed my hysterical aunt in a carl's jr parking lot while my sister was being born and my uncle was just arrested.

i found out i was going to be a big sister....again!

going to the skating rink with my sister was my jam! lol 1983

we found deer prints in the snow that came up to my sisters bedroom window. i was younger and was convinced by my sister they where footprints from one of santa's elves checking up if we were good or bad

swimming in the lake. with my sister

SIBLINGS

when i was 7 years old i met my sister for the first time. she was my half sister from my fathers first marriage. she lived with her mother in another state so i never had the opportunity to meet her before that point. i remember thinking she would have negative feelings toward me because our father left her mother. she turned out to just be the most wonderful person in the world and while i have a brother it was different, almost like getting a new sibling all at once instead of growing up with them.

my younger sister ate my dr. pepper lipsmacker, which was my favorite. i cried. later that year my mom bought me a lipsmacker necklace and i wore it everywhere.

when i was 7 my 3 year old sister died. she was diagnosed with hydrocephalia at birth. it traumatized me so bad i did not talk for a year. sorry this is sad.

SIBLINGS

when i was seven, my
parents would leave me
and my older sisters home
alone a lot. we didn't
have much in the way of
entertainment, but we had
a camcorder. so we would
take the camcorder and
prop it up on top of our
mother's curio cabinet,
move around all of our
furniture around to make
a fake talk show set, and
we filmed our own tv show
called "the stephanie
show." stephanie was
the oldest of all of us, so
of course she was the
host. she would call us
on screen and we would
assume the different
identities of her guests.
but the best part of the
whole show was that we
actually created our own
commercials. to this day,
twenty years later, we still
talk about our favorite
commercial for edible
crayons. "edible crayons!
first you color, then you eat
'em!" we only made a few
episodes of the show, but
we built bonds so strong
that to this day we're all not
only sisters but best friends
as well.

SIBLINGS

when i was seven i learned that my greatest wish would come true. i would finally be a big sister! i remember that we were in the living room when mom and dad told me. mom was sitting on the sofa and she was wearing a yellow dress that i loved because it had buttons that looked like a tic tac toe game. i don't remember it, but my parents later told me that they found me out on the porch crying that night because i didn't know what to wish for on the first star. for years i'd been wishing for a little sister or brother and now i was going to have one!

i remember jumping off my couch trying desperately to reach a balloon string as it had floated too far away. my sister walked over and calmly handed it to me. i hadn't agreed with anything she had done until that second, and a new respect was born.

i remember my heart breaking as i watched my 3 year old sister through a two way mirror at rochester school for the deaf. she needed to begin her schooling early and we had to leave her there all week because we lived so far away. they would distract her and take her into a classroom and we would go to the other room and watch to see how she adapted without us. she would cry and search for us. it was torture.

when i was seven years old, my little sister was born. this was exciting for my family. i lost my other sister two years prior due to meningitis. my parents were depressed but this new baby brought light back to their lives. i remember telling everyone in my second grade class about my new sister. i also used to pose her with my stuffed animals and take photos. even today, we are still pretty close.

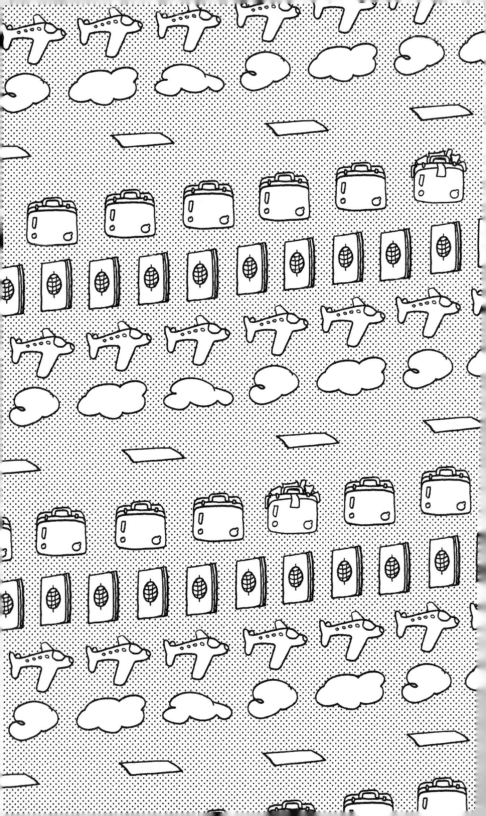

TRAVEL

my family went to disney world . it was one of the last times my mother was in decent health

i remember being at my family's cabin up north - my grandparents, parents, sister, and i would be out fishing on the lake. we would stay out for hours fishing in grandpa's spot, and we did pretty well, too. once the sun went down behind the silhouette of trees, we would all come in and make a delicious fish fry together and end the night with some type of movie - typically something along the lines of grumpy old men, blazing saddles, air plane, benny hill, or some hee haw episodes. we'd go to bed, wake up, and repeat. my heaven on earth filled with the people i loved. both of my grandparents passed just 3 weeks ago. the cabin was in our family up until this past summer since the mid 70's.

i went on an rv trip to all 50 states with my family of 7.

i was raised in an apostolic pentecostal church. the most influential people were preachers. everyone listened to preachers, preachers had all the answers. i wanted to be an evangelist when i grew up because then i would get to travel and preach! apostolic churches are unbelievably patriarchal. i didn't know that when i was 7. but being told i was not allowed to preach because girls must hold their tongue in church remains one of the top 10 most devastating things i've ever heard.

i remember when i was 7 years old we went to disney world. there was lightning ever day and my whole family got sick! still one of my favorite trips though! i loved seeing all of the movie themed rides at universal studios

my memory from when i was 7 years old was when i travelled to india. i wouldn't eat anything and got severely sick and had to be hospitalized.

TRAVEL

when i was 7 was i was a little girl. i flew to brazil for the first time to visit my mom's side of the family. i didn't know my world was never going to be the same again. after my second night there, i was robbed of my soul. my mom's cousin raped me. it didn't happen once. it went on for the next two years when he came back to america with us. my age of 7 was stollen from me. when i played barbies, i didn't want to play with anyone but myself. when i slept, i refused to sleep without my dog. my age of 7 was taken from me.

when i was 7, my parents took me to florida. all i wanted was to see disney world but we went to sea world instead.

the first time i went to visit washington d.c was when i was seven years old. i remember going to the holocaust musuem with my mother and the atmosphere there was something not easily described. i didnt understand the scope of what i was looking at back then but i knew it was something that had a big effect on my mother's eyes as well as other on lookers.

TRAVEL

my memory: i was traveling for the first time with
my parents in the balkans. one summer day, my father took us to meet his cousins in the city
of hercegnovi in montenegro. there i met nadja,
a girl of my age who i am
still friends with to this day. they had a small house, with a small library
and small
furniture. but i thought it was
quaint and perfect. their
backyard was truly something to behold. they had built a large hammock,
that was covered in lush pillows and hung from this
makeshift enclave. i laid in it with my mother as we looked up to see hundreds of grapes which
dangled above us in their hand-built vineyard. the sunlight coming
through the leaves, making the
shadows dance all over us. the vines crawled all over, and i would just
reach up to pick
as many grapes as i wanted. it was my first time
eating grapes with thick seeds. nadja and i
spent the next few hours playing in the garden with all the mediterranean cats
and climbing up trees to pick fruits. this is one of my favorite
memories from
when i was seven years old.

when i was 7 my family went to geneseo ny to visit their friends. the dad who lived there was clay young. they had a barn and in it was a horseshoe. he gave it to me. i am 63 and still have the horseshoe. it's my good luck charm.

my first trip to disneyland. my parents loaded my brother and sister into our 65 vw bug saying we were going to visit. didn't who or where just a visit. remember we didn't have to wear seat belts back then so we were playing singing and being kids when we saw through the windshield in the distance the matterhorn poking out of the trees. we asked if we could go there someday? and my dad said today is someday. we started screaming and bouncing around in the back. i can still remember how that little bug shook on the road. it was amazing

When I was seven we took a family trip to Disney world.

i went to hawaii and i got lost on the beach luckily our condo that we were staying in was right next to the beach that we were at and my parent were looking for me and eventually they came to the condo and found me, the next day we went to a different beach and my parents kept me super close to them.

my family rented a cottage on silver lake near the silver lake dunes in michigan. my dad had a small sailboat and we sailed across the lake to the dunes. we would climb the dune and then run down it as fast as we could and jump into the lake which was way over my head as there was a deep drop off due to the migrating dune sand. it was a true mixture of fear and joy! no matter how many times we did it. i wish i was 7 again. 😁

going to disney world with my grandparents, and walking around fort wilderness lodge while chip and dale jumped out of the woods!

OUTDOORS

OUTDOORS

there was a big fig tree in my front of my house the i use to hid under when i was sad and i could see out at everything but no one could see me. it made me feel like no one could ever hurt me again.

my memory from when i was 7: i lived in indonesia, and spent a day on an island crawling under the raised huts collecting sea shells and shiny pieces of trash. then we went to the docks and watched fishermen drying jellyfish that they'd pulled from the ocean.

my father was a state park ranger and we all lived in the park. the housing was central to the three camping areas. i was and still am, adventurous and i decided that i wanted to explore. several hours later my parents find me at a (strangers) family campsite eating popcorn while my parents had frantically been searching for me. i think i was grounded for quite some time.

i went to summer camp for a week when i was 7. it was my first time away from home, being in the woods, in the mountains, toasting marshmallows over a campfire, and sleeping in a cabin. the most magical part were the star gazing hikes at night "late" (past bedtime). i learned about our beautiful universe, how to look for and identify the stars, like the big and little dippers, the north star, and the seven sisters was a big one. i even saw the milky way for the first time. i wanted to become an astronomer after that. i didn't but i have a love for astronomy today and look to the night sky often and sometimes doing so brings me back to the pure joy of that moment.

when i was 7 years old i played outside at every opportunity. my curfew was to be in the house at dark. i would be ready to dash inside as i waited for the fireflies to fill the maple tree in our yard. i loved to watch that tree sparkle.

When i was seven in December of 1965, my family returned from visiting relatives in Oklahoma and the addition to our trailer was flooded. We spent the night at our neighbor's house. Our neighbor was a mailman and he would leave early for work every day. that morning he noticed that a light in the corner of the property was not on. Upon investigation we discovered that the light and the pole were gone. He moved his vehicle and as he did, the ground it was parked on washed away down the river. Our trailer was further away but that did not help, it was washed away also on December 24. I remember we lost everything and did not have much for Christmas that year. I remember the community donating clothes and toys to make our Christmas holidays better. I will never forget the pictures on the front page of the paper. what makes this so memorable, is that it was in Tucson Arizona where it does not rain much.

climbing a huge tree in my grandmothers backyard with my brother

When I was 7 I walked a mile to a summer day camp with my big sister where I made a turtle by guing small rocks onto a large rock for legs, a tail, and a head. My father kept it on his work desk until he retired. Meanwhile, Bob Dylan released Blonde on Blonde and I had no idea until 10 years later when I was 17.

my grandparents had a huge willow tree in the front yard. my grandfather would put a table and bed sheet under the hanging limbs so i could hide and play. we would make ice cream from scratch and eat it under the limbs and watch them sway and listen the the sound it made.

SuMMER

my grandparents had one of those little kiddie pools, and in the summer my cousin and i would play outside in the water all day, running around eating orange popsicles

when i was seven i spent all summer building barbie villages in our field with my dog chloe.

spending the summer at my grandparents house in norther wisconsin. nice house, on a little no named lake with another lake across the road. fishing with grandpa and my cousins. swimming in the lake. smelling that country air. so peaceful compared to the city i grew up in the rest of the year.

dancing on the back porch in to classic rock with my mom in the summer

the summer i was 7, i would often take a nap outside, on a blanket, in a tent or hammock. one day i was outside on the hammock sleeping for 6 hours, i woke up to the rain and cold. i made my way to the house drenched and my dad just laughed, my mom then told me to look at my arm. the sun tattooed diamonds on my skin from the mesh design on the hammock. it was on my face too. i was embarrassed at first, but the neighborhood kids were jealous, so i flaunted it until it faded.

flying alone as an unaccompanied minor on southwest airlines to spend the summer with my grandparents. the flight attendant sat with me and kept me safe. i was also able to take a photo with the captain in his cabin.

i remember most things from the ages of 6 to 14 as having happened all in the same year. i was molested starting at age six. the man who did this also stalked/ watched me. i remember a lot of playing in my back yard alone and talking to him through the 8 foot fence my parents put up. my childhood was actually kind of crappy. i hope you find happier memories.

the house i lived in when i was 7 had an awesome backyard. it was a *1970's* ranch style house. i remember a specific summer day. laying on the shag rug in the sun room listening to my dad blasting led zeppelin. he was grilling burgers on the back patio. when i got hot i would go slide down the slide into the pool until i was too tired. then back to the sunroom it was. it was a very average day. but i remember that day thinking "this is the life".

riding bikes during summer break.

WINTER

one of my memories when i was 7 was sledding with my brothers n sisters and being on sled with my dad going down neighbor's driveway n all way down the street, it doesn't snow nearly as much now as when i was kid and miss the serenity and beauty of the snowfall

remember spending waking hours shoveling sidewalks for quarters. i hated ice storms and corner lots. those were long days.

sliding with my brothers, but getting stuck with the silver saucer and going down the hill in circles

i live in south georgia. i remember the excitement one winter because people were saying it was going to snow. i woke up and ran to the window to find a sheet of snow in the yard. we went to school, but the teachers let us play outside until it had melted. i have not played in snow since.

walking home from the bus stop in a winter storm, my metal space-1999 lunch box in my hand. everything soft and white. no sound, just falling snowflakes.

when i was 7 i lived in manhattan and was homeschooled. i remember the winter with snow drifts piled over the garbage on the sidewalks. and that was when john lennon died

when i was 7 years old my best memory was building a snow igloo in front of our house in salt lake city utah. before there were video games and ipads.

when i was seven years old i lived in miami and it snowed... the entire backyard had a thin coating of white shiny crystals and it was unlike anything i've ever seen

Then there was the time I was sent to the store after dark. On the way I noticed a young guy working all alone at a job site, burning the garbage. I felt sorry for him, as it was winter and I imagined that he was suffering a hardship, doing that work all by himself. He called me over. I thought he wanted me to help him with something and I followed him down a ladder into the basement of the building that was under construction. Snow fell in so the first floor must not have been poured yet. He stopped me in a doorway leading to the back of the building and started to do something to my clothes. I thought he was making sure my undershirt was tucked in in case I was cold. He dug around in my pants and I was starting to think something was odd. He did not speak English, so he asked me with gestures where my penis was, and it dawned on me that he did not know about girls' genitals. I realized what he was really trying to do and I got so mad I stormed up that ladder in a fury. He tried to make me stay and I kicked at him and he let me go. He could have grabbed my legs and pulled me back down, but thankfully, he just let me leave. I don't remember if I told my parents when I got home. I just know that I forgot all about it for many years. Remembering that night suddenly, decades later, was like getting a whole new lease on life when I thought of how easily he could have raped and killed me.

FEELINGS

FEELINGS

LOVE

when i was 7 years old i started 2nd grade in a new school. i met a boy named richard and we played together every recess.
one day after school while putting on my coat, a note that he had written and put into the hood of my coat fell out.... the note simple said, "i love you." 😊

i had my first crush when i was seven years old. my 3rd grade teacher's fiance visited our class to bring her lunch and my heart felt like it would jump out of me. i kept blushing and hiding my face whenever he smiled at us. it was a scary and wonderful feeling.

FEELINGS

i told my 1st grade crush that i liked her. but she was too into shaun cassidy to care much. it was 1977 so it absolutely made sense, even if it broke my heart

second grade . . . i had such a huge crush on susie potts.
my first kiss from a girl was in the second grade. everyday after school my best friend david and i and our friend ellen would wait for our parents to pick us up. we would laugh, be silly and talk as if we were grownups. one day ellen and david were talking to each other funny, ignoring me most of the time. then ellen leaned into david and kissed him! david looked shocked! ellen just giggled. then david's mom arrived so he ran to her and they drove away. i must have looked shocked too, because ellen said don't be mad at him. then she gave me the same kiss out of pity. her mom drove up. she left leaving me alone. she thought i was jealous of david, but the truth was i was jealous of her.

When I was 7, I wanted to marry Susan Lucci.

I think I had my first crush at seven, on Jacob (not Jakob), remember playing tag with all the other kids on the playground but only really wanting to chase him.

FEELINGS

in first grade (7 years of age) i had a crush on a guy named robbie beat. completely smitten, i sat by him every day. the culmination of this crush resulted in me letting out an enormously loud fart one day while sitting next to him, resulting in everyone in the class to turn around and look. being the honorable seven year old that i was, i immediately blamed it on him, thus forever ruining our chances at a happy life together. this is my confession.

second grade. i was home sick on valentine's day, so i had to miss all the valentines being passed out. i was so embarrassed when my sister brought home this huge pink card. it was from michael. that kid had the biggest crush on me. massively embarrassing for a seven year old. looking back it was sweet, like when he gave me his mothers earrings.

i experienced my first heartbreak when i was 7, when my boyfriend (zach) broke up with me for my best friend (april). i tried to win him back on valentine's day with a paper heart and chocolates, but then he went home sick that day and the other kids said it was because of the chocolate.

the freedom and joy of being able to ride my bike away from my house, having the whole world in front of me. i didn't know how to describe the feeling at the time, but nearly 50 years later i keep searching for ways to capture that feeling from when i was 7.

FEELINGS

When   I was
7 i had my first kiss. her
name was laura and she was
2 years older than me, in addition to
being my older sister's best friend. i used to
watch the television show "seventh heaven" with
my parents, and on it one of the characters rang a
young girl's doorbell and   surprised her with a kiss.
they became boyfriend   and   girlfriend   shortly
after in the series. w h e n   i tried it, it worked for
me too. my parents didn't believe me until we were
older, when my sister confessed that she knew
that this had happened and that it was
true. we snuck away and "made
out" for a few months before
i moved later that
year.

FEAR

when i was 7 i sat up
all night listening to my
mother breathe to make
sure she didn't stop

i remember having a vivid
nightmare of my baby
shivers doll coming to life.
it became rumpelstiltskin
and tried to take my baby
sister away from me. i
had to rip his head off to
save her. after that dream i
insisted the doll be shipped
off of the philippines.

when i was 7, i was a
brownie girl scout. on days
we had meetings, i had to
wear my uniform to school.
one day a boy said, "you're
a brownie? i'm going to
eat you!" it scared the
bejesus out of me, so i quit
brownies.

I remember fearing for my
life on merry-go-rounds
and rocket swings.... but
that didn't stop me from
always jumping on them to
play!

FEELINGS

when i was 7, we lived in a new housing development in houston on a street called sandstone. and to go see one friend, i would have to ride my bike over a wooden bridge that crossed a gully called "the bayou". i once saw a big copperhead snake swimming in the bayou but i was far above it on that bridge. and i could see it. not so scary. but the part that scared me the most at that time was the occasional roar of the grasshoppers i could never see.

when i was 7, me and my family when to las vegas on vacation and on our why back we took the longer way and went though a snowy mountain and we stopped to play in the snow and there was a snow hill like 15ft my parents say and when it was time to get down i was to scared to come down so it took my mom and dad like 30mins to get me down. that's my story

my younger sister was diagnosed with type 1 diabetes when i was 7. all i knew was that she was going to have to prick her finger every day and take shots. my parents wanted to prick my finger to show me what it was like, they forced to do it. nothing couldve been scarier, but the thought thats lingered ever since is that, i'm next. what if i am next to get so terribly sick?

the year was 1994, i was 7 years old. i remember my parents watching the footage of richard nixon's funeral on tv. i had never been to a funeral and it was my first time ever seeing a coffin. i didn't understand what they were doing with it, i only knew there was a dead guy inside. my brothers, being typical older siblings, told me the coffin was going to be put under my bed. i spent the following 6 months terrified to sleep in my bed because there was a dead president under it.

FEELINGS

when i was 7 years old i was at a friend's house swimming, she lived 4 blocks from my house. after we finished swimming i git on my bike to head home. i was only wearing my swim suit abd a tshirt. i was about a block and a half from home when i got to a bit of an incline so i decided to walk my bike up the hill. as i was walking, a white van stopped abd asked me a question, which i don't remember because i was scared. i kept walking and ignoring them and they were going in reverse still bothering me. i got on my bike and rode as fast as i could to get home. i didn't go to my friends house again for several months. i always told my friend to meet me half way. i never told my dad about it until about 3 years ago. he asked me why i never said anything. i said because i was scared. i think about it every now and then. what if they had taken me? what would they have done to me? would they have killed me? or were they just trying to scare me? 37 years later, i am grateful to still be here and i am very protective of my children.

when i was 7 years old, i was living in costa rica. i was lying in bed, in the space between asleep and awake, when a tarantula crawled on my face. i screamed bloody murder and it ran away in the darkness. i'm sure it had a good laugh, but i will forever be afraid of spiders. having a dream (nightmare?) that all my teeth were falling out at the same time!

FEELINGS

When i was 7 i went to the lake with my sister who was 10. She got distracted by the cute boys on the shore so i tried to swim out to her. Before i knew it the bottom of the lake was gone, i had drifted out too far. I panicked and my body felt like it was being sucked down. My arms grasped at the sky as it disappeared clouded by the murky water. I fought my way back to the surface and gasped for air calling out my sisters name but my mouth filled with water halfway through and i was submerged again. Over and over it happened it felt like an eternity. Meanwhile on the shore a 13 yr old boy asked all the adults if they were going to do anything and when they didn't he walked in fully clothed and trudged through the muck and the water. Where i was so desperately trying to survive he was still able to touch the bottom, as he pulled me to the shore my sister finally realized what was going on and his brother swam over to help.

Keith said he would knock on my door and kiss me on the cheek. I was so terrified he'd show up that I hid in my bedroom closet the rest of the day. He never did come by the house (whew!).

GRANDPARENTS

I dug a hole in my grandparents' back yard thinking I could get to China. I was mid waist in when I hit a small round metal door. It was the happiest moment of my life and the funniest for my grandparents when they had to ~~tell~~ me it was the lid to the septic tank.

GRANDPARENTS

i remember when i was 7 years old i moved in with my grandmother and my grandfather because of her i didn't end up in an orphanage. i am so grateful for having such a wonderful woman as a grandmother and a mother to me.

when i was 7 my mom got remarried. i remember i had to go live with my grandparents for 2 weeks while my mom and new stepdad went on their honeymoon. my grandparents took my brother and i out to eat and to various fun events to take our minds off of it.

7 yr old memory- catching fish with my grandparents

when i was 7, my mom was in a psychiatric hospital for quite awhile. i lived with my grandparents, my mothers parents. i loved them both so very much. my grandmother would take me to the dome store (yes, i'm that old). she will tell the clerk we would come into the store and she'd have a full purse. when we left her pocketbook would be empty.

Living with my grandparents

GRANDMA

when it used to rain, my grandmother used to carry me on her shoulders so that i don't slip on my way to school and my clothes won't get dirty in this way.

my grandmother died when i was 7. i left the hospital one night and said "i love you, bye". "i love you" should have been the last thing i said to her. she died later that night.

when i was seven my grandmother fell down and could not get up. there was no one to help her and after hours of waiting she had to use the restroom. she was sad and embarrassed so i sat down with her.

i woke up to commotion on a cold january morning and learned that my grandma had just died.

when i was 7 i was mad at my grandmother because my grandfather had just died and i was sad and sobbing beyond belief, my first loss, my first conscious thought of death. i was mad because back at the house after the funeral my grandmother was smiling and laughing in the kitchen with others. i gave her the staredown of a lifetime. she sat me down and explained that it was better to celebrate the life that was and remember the happy times than to be angry at things out of our control. i have done this ever since..

my nana died, but her memory will live on. she was the sweetest person you will know, and i loved her more than anything. she passed away, and she had limitations, like you. her husband died, but that did not stop her from being kind and amazing. i love her, and i know that she loves me.

when i was 7, i went with my grandmother to visit my great uncle in a nursing home. i met a woman who was 103 years old, which i now realize means that she was born in 1894. imagine all the things she had lived through, the endless well of wisdom! at the time, all i could think to ask her was "did they have zippers when you were little?"

after catechism class -first time i tried hanging upside down on the monkey bars. i slipped and landed on my head. after waiting for what seemed like hours, a car pulls up with my brother and uncle from california. apparently, my great-grandmother had died.

sad memory, but a memory that i'll never forget. when i was 7 years old, my nana helen passed away from brain cancer. i was her first granddaughter. she was a fighter, but she's in a better place now.

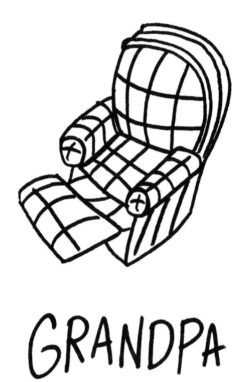

GRANDPA

i remember going to boston once a year to see my only grandparent- grandpa george. he was wonderfully tall, and as big as santa-claus. he always wore a white t-shirt and thick black frame glasses. i loved the way he talked. he had a basement and was worried me and my brother john would go down there. he would say to be careful not to wake the "bayyers" (bears) that lived downstairs. he was funny and i miss him.

GRANDPARENTS

my main male role model, my grandfather died when i was seven. at the time the impact of the event did not really hit me but looking back i deeply regret not having more time with him.

i remember my grandfathers hands. he would drive me home from school. his hands looked soft and hard at the same time. hands that went to war. hands that worked at gm to support us. he would turn the wheel, and then let it go. the wheel would turn back to its original position, and i remember the sound of the friction between the surface of the wheel and my grandfather's hands. he was one of the kindest men i've ever known. he was one of the best parts of my childhood.

i woke up the morning of my 7th birthday to find out my grandfather passed away.

when i was 7 years old, my grandpa showed me his scars from when he was a child in foster care. he went on to serve in the army, become an educator, and an elected official who was a champion for children. he inspired me to become a foster parent. my most recent placement was a 7 year old boy and 4 year old girl. their family became part of our family and we still get to babysit and spoil them! 🖤

EPIPHANY

EPIPHANY

being in second grade,
realizing for the first time
that my teacher was just a
person. and that an adult
was just a grown up kid.
broke a wall down and
i realized i could just as
easily teach myself. after
that, i immersed myself in
reading and it became my
new favorite hobby.

I discorver my true self at
age 7 and told my mother
I was meant to be a boy. I
knew back then that I was
transgender, I just didnt
know the words for it.

in first grade, my teacher,
sister mary christopher,
told me to start reading
out loud. i told her i didn't
know how to read yet.
she said, "yes, you do. go
ahead." i started, and was
so surprised when i could!
by the end of spring, i did a
reading on the altar for our
1st communion in church.
she had left our class
because she had been ill,
but she came back for it
and got to see me read. i
was a very proud 7 year
old.

EPIPHANY

it was my first day of school at a new school. i couldn't find my classroom, so i went to the principal's office and had them look me up so i knew where to go. funny enough, i ended up belonging in room 1, right across the hall, but i remember feeling really proud that i was able to figure out where i needed to go without crying or without my mom. it's one of my first memories of me really being responsible.

my mother singing camelot. the beatles. pete rose. space race. innocence. the soviet union. kennedy. became aware of the adult world.

when i was a seven year old child, i was caught kissing another man on the tv screen. after getting caught by my parents, that was when i knew i was different from other little boys. that's when i became familiar with the definition of "gay."

EPIPHANY

i went to hawaii, danced with flamingoes and discovered that the guava was the most magical fruit

when i was 7 years old i realized that i was attracted to other girls. i had a best friend named bailea and had her stay the night with me. i tried to tell my mom that i like liked her. and my mother told me, "no, honey, girls can't like other girls like that, girls and boys are supposed to be together and that's just how it is." needless to say bailea wasn't allowed to stay over again after that.

i recall being in 2nd grade, and writing a report on friends. it was the day that i realised i didn't have any.

when i was 7, my teacher was named ms. shaw. she always intrigued me because she was the first mostly androgynous person i had ever met. she was the the first girl that wasn't girly. with my family always pushing me throughout my life to be girly when i just wasn't, i remember ms. shaw was my first realization that there were other types of people in the world than girly girls and manly men. that it was okay to be different.

EPIPHANY

at age 7, i told my father (a reverend in the episcopal church), that i didn't want to go to church anymore. i said it wasn't fair that there were walls on a church when nature was already the church. i also did not agree with people sitting silent when i felt it was important for everyone to share their hearts. it didn't feel right that the church said their way was the only way when people all over knew god through their hearts. it was approx those words. my father never forced me to go again. when he was not on duty in the pulpit, he went to the beach with a handful of friends, a single chalice, his stole, a bible and some fish to cook over a fire. he had everyone share about the lesson, the ocean was the alter, the forest with birds the choir. i went to those, it finally felt accurate. i know that's not a regular 7 year old story, but that's a true story.

funny you should ask as it was a milestone in my life. i was outside playing alone with my set of metal farm animals in the dirt when this thought came into my head. if i had known the word i would have called it an epiphany. "i am a separate being. from my parents, my sister and my friends. i have unique thoughts and i can make decisions based on my experiences and not theirs.

I recall the most memorable experience at age 7 for me was telling my mother and grandmother that I was born as the wrong gender. They became my greatest supporters to being who I am today for that conversation.

is when i learned we are in a battle against good vs evil

EPIPHANY

when i started to realize
that i was different from
all the other boys at my
school

EPIPHANY

one of my most vivid memories from when i was 7 years old was painful and defining for me as a little girl. i was and am a highly sensitive person, more acutely aware of all things sensory, including intuition. this made the world as a little person difficult to navigate without adults who were understanding, compassionate, and loving. feeling very alone and overwhelmed at times i would frequently cry and become upset. this is where as a 7 year old my own father became incredibly angry at me for wanting to be comforted over a nightmare that frightened me and he very clearly let me know that he thought i was "crazy"....this changed me right then and there... i was immediately aware that sharing your vulnerabilities and needing and asking for support and comfort was now a way to be deeply scorned and rejected...ouch.

when i was 7 years old i had a vision of my future. i knew i would have a pet snake. my soul mate would share the same birthday as me. july 1st. i would die at 25...the last part freaked me out and i ran to tell my father. a part of me believed it to be true as i grew older. i had a pet snake in my 20s. i think i met one of my soul mates with my birthday in college. well i am 30 now. i did die metaphorically at 25 when i had a spiritual awakening. death can also be symbolic of rebirth. i was granted the gift of vision. to see beyond the veil. spirits, angels, ancient mythological teachers in many forms. they conducted healing work through me on individuals and the planet as a whole. i stepped into a realm of knowledge that was unfamiliar to me. intriguing and frightening at the same time. today i am forever changed. i don't share this story with just anyone. i have so many experiences to share but i'm not sure that the world is ready. i'll just continue to paint them in my artwork.

FOOD

FOOD

When I was 7, it snowed at Camp Lejeune. All of the kids in the neighborhood came to sled in our front yard, churning it into mud. My mother leaned out the front door and yelled to everyone to GO HOME -- and bring back two slices of bread. That was the day she made french toast for the whole neighborhood. It was perfect.

When I was 7 years old I loved eating an ice- cream from the vender that came by with the ice-cream machine;

When i was 7 my cousin and i would walk around the lake to the store with our 50 cents and get penny candy. it would come in a little brown paper bag. we had 50 pieces of candy. We were so excited!

helping grandma cook sunday dinner for the big family. i was so short and burnt my arm on the stove since i couldn't quite reach. i still have the scar 38 years later. i loved cooking with her. this is one of my most cherished memories.

i remember going to the local restaurant for lunch with my grandma and getting 25 cents worth of penny candy. a swedish fish here and a tootsie roll there. 25 cents never went so far!

i had this awakening when i was 7 as if it just occurred to me that i was suddenly seeing the world in a new and bigger way. it took place in the parking lot of jackson's ice cream in dania, fl which i remember because up until that day, i had always loved and asked for bubblegum ice cream. that day i got mint chocolate chip. i've gotten mint chocolate chip ever since.

FOOD

shelling peas with my grandmother

my grandmother lived up the hill from a candy store. one day i came outside to find my older sister and my cousin sitting in grandma's gravel driveway, eating the biggest sweet tarts i had ever seen - they were palm sized. and they wouldn't share. i asked where they got them and they told me they had found them growing in the gravel. one by one i must've moved every rock in that driveway, ending up with bloody fingertips before they fessed up. i told my own kids that story nearly ten years ago, and they still hold it over my sister's head.

i had asthma add a kid. i remember a nun at the catholic hospital sneak lollipops to me after my allergy shots.

feeling "cool" eating pixie stix :)

when i was seven my dad was digging a big hole in our back yard. being the helpful kid i was, i picked up a shovel and started to "help" him. we dug down about three feet deep before we hit a piece of junk. it was rubbery and flesh colored and all around unsettling. we got it out of the hole and it turned out to be a latex mask of a boy. i didn't have any siblings at the time, but in my 7 year old mind, that mask was the left over face of my dead brother that died before i was born. i was so freaked out, i thought my parents were children eaters. i starved myself for 3 days, and by the end of the third day, i broke down in tears. imagine the look on my mom and dads face when i had to confess i wasn't eating bc i didn't want to get fate enough for my family to kill me and eat me.

going door to door selling firewood with my father and being paid with doughnuts and chocolate milk. i was the richest kid in the world on payday!

FOOD

my
grandmother   was
visiting   us   in   my   mom's
apartment one day. later during the
day, it was just me and her preparing to
bake a cake. my mom had gone to the grocery
store to buy missing ingredients for the cake, and
had been gone for a while. i was getting anxious
waiting for her to return. that's when my grandmother
turned to me and advised me to use magic to bring her
back. "let's cast a spell together to bring her back" she
said. i then closed my eyes and focused all my strength
to my fingers, where it felt like my blood was about to
explode from my fingertips. after our little seremony
was done i asked my grandmother if it had worked.
"i don't know" she replied, "have you checked
outside?" i then looked out the window and saw
my mother on the sidewalk beneath me,
casually strolling to the apartment
complex   with   a   grocery
bag in   hand.

FOOD

when i was 7 i visited the white house with my parents. i was really into grape bubblicious gum at that time. i was chomping on two pieces and managed to blow a bubble as big as my head... right in front of the secret service. i got the meanest glare from them and to this day i am still scared of the secret service.

when i was 7 years old i went to the hospital for the first time. i hit my head on a play kitchen set after falling backwards in a rocking chair. i had to get five staples to close the wound. i remember my dad bringing me a blueberry muffin afterwards and letting me draw on his pda. that made me feel a lot better.

when i was 7, i met my best friend. on her birthday her mom made pink cupcakes for everyone and she ended up throwing up all over the classroom. i had never seen neon pink vomit so i went over to her and declared her my best friend

i got in trouble for knocking over a jar of cocoa and not cleaning every morsel of cocoa up.

2 memories 1)helping my grandmother with making pancakes for breakfast. 2) picking up pecans from the trees in my grandmother's backyard.

i remember this one time during the summer, me, my sister, my little brother and my mom were sitting outside under our old clothes line, at this big red wooden picnic table. we had just got done playing in the sprinkler and mom brought out lunch. we had peanut butter and jelly sandwiches with chips and milk. to this day that is my favorite memory and pb&j's are still the best.

when i was seven years old i had a thomas the tank engine birthday party. my cake had peanuts and we learned my friend had a peanut allergy.

when i was seven, my dad offered me a budweiser to try a sip of it. he told me it was "sparkling apple juice". i took a big swig, and immediately spit it all over him, my uncle, the table and floor. then i was sent to get some rags to clean up or else i would be grounded.

ANIMALS

my mom got remarried
and my new father lived
in the country, on a small
acreage. moving into
the new place was a big
change from our small
apartment in the city. i
loved being free to explore,
and i was particularly
fascinated by the frogs
and tadpoles in our pond.
i would love to catch them,
and chase my sisters
away with them. one time i
caught a big one, and put
it in a sand pail so i could
play with it later. coming
back at the end of the hot
day, i found a desiccated,
gruesome-looking, dead
frog. i'll never forget it.

i went up the roof on a
ladder, i was a little trouble
maker, and there was a
nest of little baby chicks,
they were hairless and
looked disgusting and
they fell on my head, i
screamed like a little girl
and my dad still reminds
me to this day.

one of my first memories
being that age is getting
on for a horseback riding
lesson for the first time.

went to a cattle auction
with my grandpa and
wanted him to buy a bull
calf. he got a large bull.
on the way home i got mad
at him and insisted he stop
the truck so i could ride
in back with the bull. i got
more upset because he
wouldn't let me.

when i was 7 years old we
moved from colorado to
california. it was our third
movebin three years. i had
this huge stuffed lion that
i treasured because i won
it at a fair. as we packed
up the car to drive away
my dad told me i had to
leave the lion at the curb
because it was too big to
fit in the station wagon with
my parents, three siblings,
our dog & cat, and myself.
i still remember looking out
the back window driving
away from my lion and
feeling devastated. like i
was leaving my childhood
and treasure in colorado.
as i grew up from there,
many people called me an
"old soul." i think it was that
moment that defined me.

my dad teaching me how to
ride a horse 🐴

ANIMALS

every year at my school we held a carnival. i tried winning a goldfish and ended up with 5! my mom graciously let me keep them all, but only 2 survived. those fish taught me about cannibalism.

when i was 7 we still lived in northern california not far from sanfransisco and one of my memories was joining friends in wading around in the creek and catching & releasing different sized & colored salamanders 🤓

I was seven
years old when I
got chased by an ostrich.

ANIMALS

when i was 7 i loved
this stupid bunny stuffed
animal, i beamed him hairy
the rabbit. and i refused
to leave the house with
out him. when my parents
started to fight i would just
sit under the covers of my
bed talking to him about
how sad it was. but on the
first day of school i brought
him in my backpack and
a kid found him and threw
him into the ground and
tore harry in two. i tried to
put him back together but
i couldn't find the stuffing.
he just sat for years now
in my closet maimed and
forgotten.

when i was seven we
grew up on a property of
four acres. my brothers
and sisters and i would
play outside for hours.
we had a woods, a creek,
an orchard, and a huge
garden. one day we found
two baby bunnies in that
garden and brought them
to the house. we took care
of them. we loved them
but one day daddy said we
had to let them go. we did
but we were heartbroken.
but... every once in a while,
when we were out weeding
the garden, there they
would be! and sometimes
they would hop along and
follow us in the rows!

ANIMALS

when i was 7, i got my first pet: a rabbit i had named pellets. i have strong memories of pellets playing with my sister's dog dottie when she was a puppy. those animals were with me throughout my childhood and into my teenage years, forming the major role that animals and their welfare have played in my life.

my pet bird peepsy flew away and left my family heartbroken... 🏠

my dad got stationed to germany just after my seventh birthday, and my grandmother decided to join us overseas. she didn't have much time to get me a gift during the move, so one day we took a whole day trip to munich to get a steiff pony, which i still have 33 years later.

i lived on a farm. we would fish for snapping turtles, play in hay mounds, pick fresh chickens eggs, taunt the bull next door, and sled down the hills on the barn yard. it was a great life!

when i was 7, i was stung all over my arms and hands by bees after stepping on one in an open field. it was also the first time i ever used a classic rotary phone. a friend's mother helped me and it was her kitchen phone. i'm 41 now and i remember that day vividly.

when i was seven, i found a ladybug inside my house. i was so excited that i picked him up and decided to take him on a ride on my tricycle! i proudly rode my plastic tricycle around the playroom with the ladybug high above my head on the tip of my finger. after a few laps i checked my finger and to my surprise, the lady bug was no longer there. i searched and searched the playroom until finally i found him! to my despair, he was no longer a cute crawly insect, but a flattened piece of shell on the bottom of my plastic tricycle tire. he must have fallen off and landed underneath my path:(i cried for a few hours

i got a duck for easter

ANIMALS

When I was seven I had this polar bear. His name is Polar. We were best friends and we still are.

i was 7 in 1988 and we lived in panama. we had an old vw camper and would go beach camping on the weekends. one time as we headed home we were driving through jungle and my mom swore she say a monkey. my dad didn't believe her so he pulled over and put a left over cupcake on a tree stump by the edge of the road and we sat in the car as still and quiet as we could. after about 5 minutes monkeys started to come from every where in the jungle and fight over the cupcake. in my mind there were thousands, though it was probably more like tens, of little spider monkeys everywhere. i can still picture the little pink cupcake being mauled by all those monkeys 😊

When I was 7, I used to dream of being a veterinarian. I really love animals.

I grew up outside of Yellowstone National Park. One night in the very early pre-dawn hours, my mom woke me up and brought me down to the livingroom of the cabin to look out the big picture window. I squinted out against the darkness, tired and a little grumpy wondering why she had dragged me out of bed. As the stillness of the night gathered around us, I saw a flash of...something swooping down from a nearby pine tree attacking the birdseed bell my mom had put up the day before. I focused more closely, trying to get a better understanding of what I was seeing. It landed on the bell and was still for a moment and it all gelled: it was a flying squirrel! So glad my mom thought it was important enough to wake me up, to share that silent moment of wonder with her, to witness the strange nocturnal ramblings of a weird flying rodent. Nature is cool.

getting a live bunny for easter that i named suzy.

ANIMALS

we lived for a few
years in the angeles
national forest in a
small place named
chilao. it was home
to campgrounds,
a ranger station,
rattlesnakes and other
wildlife. my older
brother and i talked
our young 4 yr old
sister into wading into
the waste water ponds
at the ranger station
to capture some pet
frogs who happened to
be mating and laying
eggs. we brought them
home and put them
in the bathtub. when
my mom came home
she had to deal with
a bathtub full of frog
eggs. i remember she
filled up an aquarium
and we watched them
hatch and develop
into frogs. i have
always appreciated
my mother's optimistic
attitude in dealing
with challenges. this
was the first time
as a young child i
recognized that quality
in her that i admire
most.

ANIMALS

i was at my aunt and uncle's house and they were slaughtering chickens that day. i was watching my aunt chopping off chickens heads with a hatchet on a stump and throwing the headless chickens. we would make a game out of trying to chase them. one of the headless chicken started chasing me and keeping up with me. i would dodge one way it would follow i would dodge the other way and it would follow. it got so close i got blood in the back of my leg! needless to say i never chased headless chickens again!

When I was in first grade. We lived in Northern California and my mother had rented a small house on a horse ranch not far from Cotati. I had a friend named Autumn & we took turns riding her Pinto pony in the corral, doing chores and grooming the Arabians which were beautiful spirited horses.

there were two solid white twin calfs born on the ranch next to ours. brauma bulls. they were shown at the omak stampede, and rodeo in eastern washington.

ne of my best memories is of my favorite pony named scotch

ANIMALS

I grew up on the NW side of Chicago, 21 blocks from Lake Michigan in a two flat owned by my Polish grandma, my Busia. We loved sitting on the benches of our front porch on summer evenings and discuss hopes, dreams and the day's events with each other and passing neighbors. One such evening, when I was 7 years old, we were startled by the blazing sirens of an oncoming police car that screeched to a halt across from our house. Two stern officers exited the vehicle and rushed down the gangway, pounded the door and entered our new neighbor's home. We didn't know much about these new neighbors only that they had lots of kids and just moved up here from Mexico City. The officers didn't stay long, but as they walked back up to their car they were laughing quite hysterically. Busia looked at me, smiled and said, "Something else is going to happen and it's going to be good!" Well, 15 minutes later, 5 cops returned with a squad car and a patty wagon. They went into the house and 4 came back straining as they hoisted a 400 pound PIG down the long sidewalk and into the paddy wagon. The last officer carried a rooster which joined his farm mate in the wagon. It seems our neighbors had no idea that raising farm animals was illegal in Chicago city limits. I was relieved to discover I wasn't totally going crazy because every morning at sunrise since they moved in, I was awakened by crowing!

ANIMALS

CAT

i used to have a cat named tom and i would love to kiss his nose. one day i kissed his nose but he wasn't in the mood and scratched the left side of my face. i calmly walked into the house and looked in the mirror. i was bleeding a lot and as i tried to clean myself up, i realized the bleeding wasn't stopping and i would have to tell my mom. i ended up getting 20 stitches to the left side of my face. not sure how i was so calm during all of that. yes, i was 7!

after my parents divorced i had to move and switch schools midyear. not long after, my cat followed me on my walk there one morning. being the new kid, i enjoyed the attention she brought while we waited to go inside. and, being the new kid, i was mortified when she, too, ran inside. even more so when i was later called down to the principal's office to "claim" her.

ANIMALS

here is my 7 year old memory: my step brother and i shared a bedroom. we had a white, adopted fatcat named tc, stood for top cat. this cat would only pee on my brothers bed by his feet, never anyone else's bed. since the mattress would need to be cleaned in the basement. we would ride the mattress down our the stairs from the top floor. there were 2 staircases and a landing. we rode the mattress down as many times before we were yelled at to stop. we actually looked forward to when the cat would pee on his bed because we had so much fun!

when i was seven, my hamster and i didn't get along. my babysitter's sister's cat had kittens. i traded my hamster for a little black kitten. she became my best friend, now i only adopt black cats! my hamster loved my baby sitter.

memory- watching my cat have 2kittens.

in 1997 i got my cat, baxter. we drove an hour away to a ragdoll breeder and i met him, my little white fluff ball, seeing his fluffy white older brother with peachy highlights, who he would look exactly like as an adult. we put him in a towel-lined banker's box and started driving home. my mom asked me what i wanted to name him, just as we passed one of those manufacturers that's out in the illinois countryside, baxter. being 7, i immediately said that i would name him baxter. at the time, the meow mix commercial with the song and the cat of the same name was on tv, so we all proceeded to sing the meow mix song to my little kitten in his banker's box. he was my best friend and i loved him for 17 years, and he passed away in 2014 while i was at college, christmas 2013 was our last one together. there will never be a replacement for him.

ANIMALS

DOG

when i was 7 i came home from school and saw an enormous box just inside the front door. then i heard a noise. just as i was peering over the side of the box a little creature jumped up and i immediately thought wow my mom got us a lion cub. then i looked again and realized that fluffy head was a puppy. that was the day i met our dog sparky.

when i was 7, my mom bought a dog. i remember playing outside with him on that very first day and thinking that i had never been happier in my life. i'm 22 now and the dog is still around. he's part of the family

i lost my favorite siberian husky kiska an amazing fluffy dog who was my best friend from birth. no dog could ever replace that dog.

ANIMALS

when i was seven, my mother rented a camp on oneida lake in new york. one day we wereout on the dock with my dog bruce, an english springer spaniel. bruce get so excited and was barking so hard, he backed off of the dock and learned to swim the hard way!

when i was 7 my dog bit my pinkie off

I had a dog named Bear

when i was 7 my favorite movie was "101 dalmatians". i got my first dog, that year, from santa clause. she was a dalmatian and i named her patches.

While walking our female dog who was in heat I momentarily got distracted at the playground, turned around to find a male mounting poor Coco on the end of the leash.

i remember getting a puppy when i was 7 years old. it was one of the happiest days of my life

i remember dance classes (jazz) and my dogs, mollie and sadie) the most from when i was 7.

my dog petey was hit by the ups man in the summer of '79. nobody cleaned the blood and brains off the road so i was forced to see it every day until the rains washed it away. my mom kept his body in a box in the back of our station wagon for a week before burying him and i was forced to smell his decompo

when i was seven years old...my daschund named schnitzel ran away. i was an only child and he was my best friend. i went to a parochial school and believed in god. on the 3rd morning he was not back and i prayed harder than i ever had that schnitzel would be safe and come home to me. when i got off the bus at home that afternoon, mom opened the door and out he came running into my arms. at that moment i absolutely believed in god and in prayer.

ANIMALS

i was attacked by a neighbor's akita dog (not on leash) in my front yard and had to get 13 stitches cause it tore my back up pretty bad.

as a child my best friend was my dog wrollo. wrollo loved rubber balls, unfortunately once he nabbed one, it broke. my neighbors children would at ball in their yard a d the dog would always get the stay ball. one day while he was on the act of grabbing the ball their mom. threw a bucket of water on the dog. a few weeks later i threw a bucket of water on the mom because the dog couldn't....in my mind it was the golden rule. do into others as others do into you. needless to say my dad had a long talk with me about the golden rule.

i did a silly dance to amuse my cousin's dog

i remember that my mom and i bought a puppy from the humane society. it's name was davey. he was the sweetest dog. i guess either my mother didn't want to take care of it anymore or we couldn't afford to take care of him anymore because we were very poor, but she made me go with her to return him after a few months. i remember i cried and cried. i'm pretty sure it felt as if someone had died. i'll never forget driving away from him and feeling so terrible. i guess that's why i own so many animals now.

my family rescued a pomeranian from the highway that year. it had been shaved in random spots all over. we named it lucky. my younger sister actually almost died trying to rescue it. she jumped out of the car on the highway and two older people helped her catch it. my parents ended up rehoming it.

riding my bike with the banna seat and my bassett hound named tippi in the basket on the front of the bike. going all over the neighborhood. morning to evening

i picked out my dog, max, from a litter by him being so excited to meet me that he jumped on me and knocked me down and started licking my face.

playing with my dog named whiskey

scarred for life, on vacation in minocqua, wi, our three year old golden retriever buster was hit by a car and killed. it was 1985.

when i was seven i had begged and begged my parents for a puppy for as long as i could remember. that was the year they finally caved in and my dad took my brother and i out to petco one day to pick out a rescue dog. we picked out the perfect one and i named her daisy. when we brought her home she was so hungry that she ate two whole bowls of food. she was the sweetest dog ever and she loved my dad, like she knew he was the head of the pack! it's now 16 years later and that is one of my most cherished memories with my dad. he passed away last year, but my old dog is still here to remind me of him.

PALS

PALS

when i was 7 years old, i was just going back to public school from being home schooled for a year and a half. i walked into my 3rd grade english classroom and my eyes locked with a girl who i played with a lot in kindergarten and first grade. she lit up with the biggest smile i've seen in my life and i was just as happy to see her. we are still good friends to this day, 20 years later.

i met my husband at age 7. we were in mrs. kubacki's class together. before our 3rd grade year he moved away. 18 years later i re-met him, and in that same week i graduated college and started my 1st teaching job. he claims when we were 7, i chased him on the playground and kissed him. i don't recall that, but i let him keep the faith. our kids give great belly laughs when their dad reminisces. 20 years later we are super happy and i still teach art ♡

when i was 7, my best friend and i, as we awaited our dads to pick us up from school played in the rain as if there were no tomorrow. we played and laughed and hugged goodbye as 7 years do. the next day, jerome's seat next to me lay empty. my teacher pulled me aside and whispered, "jerome is no longer with us". jerome had died the night before from an asthma attack. i have never gotten over empty chairs. i am 52 years old and i am greatful to tell the story for the first time. thank you.

i met my life-long best friend, debbie when i was 7. she and i would sing to the song hair (from the musical of the same name) as we whipped our hair in all directions. no worries, cares!

playing stickball with my neighborhood friends until the streetlights went out on a hot, humid summer night. running fast cooled us off - we thought!

PALS

when
i was 7 my
best
friend
cindy
taught
me to
ride a
bike.
i was
scared
to death
so she
brought
me on
top of a
hill and
said, "i
won't let
go just
pedal,
i've got
you" so,
i did. i
pedaled
down
the
entire
hill and
then i
looked
back
and saw
cindy, she
was still
standing on
the top of the hill.

PALS

When I was seven years old I made a friendship bracelet for my best friend. She awkwardly said she didn´t want it... because she had a new best friend.

when i was 7, i remember all the fun my friends and i would have riding bikes and skateboards around the neighborhood.

when i was 7 years old, i was sat next to a boy named zachary in class. he liked the way i drew and asked me to teach him to draw a mermaid. he was trying to get my attention or ask me something about his mermaid but i was preoccupied with something else, so he tried to poke me with his pencil to get my attention and i stood up, so he poked my butt with the pencil tip. i shot my hand up yelling to my teacher "mr. barker! zachary poked my butt!" he got in trouble and had to stay in at recess. i felt bad, and stayed in with him. he became my best friend for over ten years. we fell out of touch for a few years after we turned 18, but we have been hanging out again lately, and it feels like no time has passed at all. "mr. barker, zachary poked my butt" is a phrase we still say to this day.

PALS

When I was 7 my best friend was Samantha. Our apartments were right next door. We had a club house under her dining room table where we held secret meetings. That table was right next to the grand piano and her grandmother Mrs Kriebel, who was a retired concert pianist would supply a lovely soundtrack to our clubhouse meetings. It was a time of calm amid much chaos for both, as she had been abused and I had already lived through my father's 1st suicide attempt and trip to the psych ward. Friends are often the salve to wounds we weren't even aware needed healing.

My family moved from St Paul to Amery, WI. My heart broke when I told my best friend, Shannon. I still remember our tear-streaked faces reflecting in the mirror when we snuck out to the bathroom to cry. It remains one of my most bittersweet memories. Children need their best friends in their lives, even at age seven.

when i was 7, i would ride my my bike around my neighborhood with my friends for hours. we would race, do tricks, ride down to the lake, play tag, etc.

when i was 7, we moved to wurtsmith air force base in oscoda, michigan. we lived temporarily in a trailer right next to the runway where c-130s, bombers, and fighter jets took off. the whole trailer would shake and we often had to hang onto items to prevent them from falling and breaking. on the first day of school, i met another girl who also lived in the trailers and rode my bus. it turned out that she was in my class. and, when we finally got housing, we were placed on the same block on the base. we became lifelong friends. i still talk to her 35 years later.

wes, tony, scott and i playing hide and go seek in the hot kansas air- carefree and perfectly happy as long as we were with each other every waking moment.

PALS

i had a best friend. we used to dress up in little house on the prairie dresses and bonnets. she had cystic fibrosis and was not expected to live long. she was also so so spoiled..even taking a bath with her, she would sit at the deeper end and gather all of the bubbles and pull them to her side. we would buy matching shoes and she would start taking mine home when hers got worn. she would take things of mine home. despite all that difficulty, i miss her madly. she passed away just after having her second daughter, while working as a pulmonologist. a lesson in loving people as they are.

when i was 7 years old my best friend jessica and i used to have sleepovers. we would wear her pokemon slippers and jump on her trampoline early in the morning. and her mother would make us rubarb pancakes.

When i was seven i met my best friend and we are still fiends 28 years later.

when i was seven years old i met the best friend i've ever had. we were at the bus stop, (and being the socially awkward person i am), i tried to strike up a conversation about skunks. it was extremely awkward, but i guess that doesn't matter because she's still my best friend today and she probably always will be

Evee (Evelyn) was my best friend. We met in 2nd grade in September, and we were inseparable. We made up games and painted our nails and shared secrets. I remember cutting through the woods to get to her place after school. Then, at Christmas, she got a bunny. He was super cute and loveable. But he wasn't allowed where she lived. Her mom decided they should move. 20+ miles away – another world when you're 7. We had every intention of staying in touch, but I never saw Evee again.

PALS

i got separated from my best friend on the first day of school. we held on to each other and they had to pull us apart. we were crying.

APPEARANCE

APPEARANCE

it was *1970*...and i was a quite thin 7 year old girl (okay, skinny is more definitive) starting first grade. in homemade clothes. everyone else (it seemed) had found the latest fashions and were proudly showing them off. store bought clothes for me were two things. (1) unaffordable (2) i'll-fitting. i never felt accepted until i found out that humor was the key to breaking through the silent, judgmental stares. i've used it throughout my 53 years. p.s. i'm no longer skinny ;)

I WAS WEARING MY PINK DRESS WHEN THE SCHOOL PHOTO WAS TAKEN.

at 41 years of age, one memory of my 7-year-old self not only dominates that year, but my childhood. it was the first time i was told i was sexy. he was a teenaged son of my father's friend. he babysat my brothers and i while our parents went on doubledates. he told me i was his secret girlfriend and explained what girlfriends do.

when i was 7, a friend of my mom's told me that i was such a pretty girl. i did not correct him & and say i was a boy. oddly enough, it excited me to get such a nice compliment.

at 7 years old i was obsessed with growing taller. from age 7 onward i kept personal track of my height with the wall in my closer. by the time my family and i had moved out of my childhood home when i was 13 i had grown over a foot tall. it was one of my favorite things about my room.

one of my funnies memories from when i was seven, is being so jealous of my best friend's long ponytails. her hair was was so long and straight, mine so pouffy and curly. i pulled them constantly, and blamed someone else every time. didn't tell her it was me until years later! lol

i remember my school picture and how i thought i was so ugly red hair ,black eye brows,big teeth, freckles and a ugly plaid shirt.....

wearing a clip on tie to public school and having it pulled off by another kid.

trying to fit in in school being one of the only white kids

i was born with a cleft lip and pallet. i remember having all sorts of doctors appointments getting me ready for a surgery i was going to have. they tested my hearing and i had to drop little wooden blocks into a yellow bucket whenever i heard a beep in my headphones.

My mother only dressed me in frilly dresses and flat shiny pleather shoes, because "That's what girls wear". But I hated it, and constantly begged for jeans so I could play kickball, like the other girls in school. She finally caved, and got me a pair of light blue jeans and a pair of white cowboy boots. I went to school the next day wearing both of them, and confidently walked up to a group of kids to join their game, like I was an action hero in a movie. They laughed at me, told me no, and kicked dirt at me. My new pants were filthy, and I ended up getting punished by my mother for not keeping them clean. She only let me wear leggings after that.

GLASSES

i got straight a's that year, which was amazing since i had not been diagnosed with near- sightedness, and could not see the blackboard very well: the first eye exam and glasses did not come til 4th grade. my favorite place was,and still is, avon by the sea beach at the nj shore, and my swim lessons at the ymca made me brave enough to be able to swim in our pool and my ocean!

when i was seven, i got my first pair of glasses. i was so excited to be able to finally see! but when i looked in the mirror, i looked different with the glasses on. a few hours after i got the glasses, i admitted to my mother that i was nervous about going to school the next day. i wasn't afraid of being made fun of, but i was afraid no one would recognize me. my mother laughed and told me that wouldn't happen, that i still looked like myself but just with glasses on. still i was worried, but she was - of course - right.

when i was 7, i was seven years old and i got my first pair of glasses. now i am 24, and never had a day passed that i didn't go out without glasses. the result was that i only have a vague idea of what i look like without glasses.

when i was 7 years old, second grade, i had a severe lisp. when i tried to say words like "church" and "soldier," i said "shursh" and "sholsher." the thing that sticks in my mind is that i had to go to speech therapy when all the other kids went to recess. on the bright side, my diction is exceptional now. :)

i remember wearing a corrective eye patch for my long gone lazy eye, and someone on the playground called me a pirate. i screamed back, "pirates don't have smiley faces and hot air balloons painted on their eye patches. jeez! get it right."

APPEARANCE

When I was 7, I got my first pair of glasses. I was really
excited at the time, not only because I could see things
that I didn't realize normal people could see, but
I also thought of it as a "new look" and maybe I
wouldn't be picked on at school as much. After
going to school later that week, it was clear that
the glasses only made me more vulnerable.
The next day, I left my house with my
glasses on to make it seem like I was
fine wearing them (for my Mom), but as
I walked to the bus stop, I took them
off and put them in my pocket. I
was picked on at school still,
but not for my glasses that
day. Walking home from the
bus stop that day, I took
my glasses out of my
pocket and put them
back on as if the
whole time I was
wearing them
and nothing
has hap-
pened.

APPEARANCE

my
mem-
ory from
when i
was 7: as
a family we
were watching
"i love lucy" on tv
and something funny
happened but i didn't
laugh cause i couldn't
really see it. when i say
closer to the tv my parents
noticed i would really laugh.
so they took me to the eye dr
and i ended up getting glasses.
when i got them i balled in the car.
my parents tried to figure out why i was
crying, i finally got out the words"because
i know jeremy will make fun of me behind
my back" between sobs. i had heard how a
friend of mine talked about "4 eyed" people after
they were out of ear shot and i didn't want to be
laughed at.

HAIR

my mom gave me s pixie hair cut before the first day of school. everyone thought i was a boy. i deliberately wore a dress every day for the rest of the school year

when i was 7 years old, my mom forced me to get a haircut and i cried about it for a very long time.

when i was, i got my haircut short to look like my sister's best friend. strangers thought i was a boy and when i went to mcdonald's i cried because they gave me the boy's toy without asking which one i wanted even though i preferred the hot wheels cars to the barbie dolls.

APPEARANCE

when i was in 2nd grade
i had a horrible haircut
with a 6 inch rat tail and
my two front adult teeth
grew in before i lost the
rest of my baby teeth. my
teacher used to celebrate
one student a week where
the rest of the class had to
write something nice about
them on the blackboard.
one of the comments was
from a boy in my class
who use to call me toots.
he wrote "i like your buck
teeth" that is the only thing
i remember about 2nd
grade.

when i was 7, i got a "shag"
haircut, the first time i
remember taking part in
any kind of fad or trend. it
was 1973. i was so proud
of my haircut! the same
day i got it, i was waiting
in the car and i saw a boy
smiling and waving at me.
that was also a first! he
walked closer, and i saw
the look on his face turn
to disgust, and he said, "i
thought you were mike! but
you're a girl, ugh!" i was so
embarrassed!

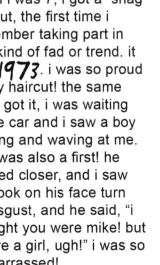

PLAYTIME

PLAYTIME

i remember being at recess and swinging really high, then jumping off the swing

when i was 7, i lived in an old farm house with a barn. i felt so free, listened and danced to the lion king soundtrack, rode horses, played in the creek and loved to feel the sun and wind in my hair. that house was built in 1815 and was recently torn down.

we were living in my great grandmothers 4th floor attic. i would lay awake at night with a little flashlight and count the nails poking through the ceiling.

when i was 7 my grandmother wouldn't let me play with the other neighborhood kids. so instead i'd be restricted to playing in her backyard alone. i instead made friends with the neighborhood stray cats that would vist me while i ran between the sheets drying on the clothesline, picked flowers and hunted for insects.

one of the many memories i remember most at 7 years old is loving to swing on the swing set and hanging upside down from the seat- that was always fun for me☺! i was a crazy tree climber too.

when i was 7 i can remember playing with those toy plastic dinosaurs whenever i could

i remember working up the courage to ask to play with the other kids in mcdonald's playroom and getting quickly and remorsefully told no by a little girl.

i had these disney princess dolls and when i was 7 we went to disney world and got the princesses to sign my dollsonce we got them signed my mom made a shadow box and put the dolls in them in it

i used to go to my grandfather's amusement park in scranton, pa. i used to ride the rides all day for free. best memories.

my friend katie and i used to surf down the stairs of her old farmhouse until her mom would catch us. we had so much fun!

Skates and bikes and mudcakes in the back yard. Flip Wilson and HeeHaw on the tube... black and white, literally. Where's Vietnam and making drawins of Nixon in the daily paper. Fun with my brothers and sisters on the front stoop....hitting the sack at sundown. Innocence and great memories. Family is big but still lonely.

when i was 7, i walked out to my swing set to find a snake curled up under my swing. i was scared and couldn't swing. i asked my uncle (who was watching me) to do something about it but he was scared too. so my uncle played barbies with me. it was a good day.

playing at the beach on lake michigan.

i remember my cousin betting me i couldn't climb up at 30 ft rope. proved her wrong, but it took a lot of coaxing to get me down...

riding in wagon being pulled by a four wheeler

a memory i have when i was seven was running out to the street after school and everybody putting their shoe in the middle to see who was "it" inka binka bottle of inka!

falling into a lake and being fished out by my parents.... then being scolded for not being more careful. ☺

PRETEND

when i was seven i would play with my neighbor michelle. we both had imaginary friends (genie and dexter) and the four of us would play together every day. we still talk about it to this day

when i was 7 years old, my favorite memory was playing batman and robin with my sisters out on our farm. i was for sure going to marry dick grayson one day cause he was so dreamy!

PLAYTIME

erin and i had a spy agency

when i was seven years old my parents gave me a treehouse. it had a rope on a pulley with a bucket tied to the end of the rope. the treehouse also had a trap door. i would climb up into my treehouse and i would pretend i was a pirate. i would put my white miniature poodle in the bucket and tie him off half way down from the tree house. he was my lookout. his name was stash.

When I was 7, I climbed a wall that ran the length of my driveway. I thought it a mean dragon whose back I fearlessly ran across. I felt invincible. Upon returning years later, I saw the wall in its true, diminutive height. The ghost of that little girl ran up to me and told me that I was still invincible. I have slayed many walls since then.

this is me at 7. i wanted to be evil knevil so bad my grandma made me this shirt and i had my grade school picture taken in it.

my favorite memories when i was 7 is when my sister and i would walk up and down grandma's driveway pretending to shop, visit imaginary friends (my friend's name was bloody mary), and visit my sister's imaginary zoo which was a high rise tower with different animals on every level. grandma's driveway was about a quarter mile of gravel road. on our way home an imaginary 18 wheeler would drive behind us with all of our shopping finds. then we would get on the old metal swing set (which was an airplane) and fly to disneyland and other wonderful places.

I used to love dressing up as a kid, and when I was 7, I was all about ninjas! I used to take a shiny orange table runner (like a long ornate cloth) and wrap it around myself. I also had red sunglasses, a toy dagger, and cardboard throwing stars. As I look back at old photos of me at this age, I think to myself: "I still want to be a ninja, because ninjas have so much fun!"

PLAYTIME

i lived in a tiny town in east texas. i loved dinosaurs and i was convinced that summer that i was going to excavate my first dinosaur. all summer, i worked on the same hole. one day, i hit a blue dinosaur bone! i was so excited! i ran inside to tell my mom and she freaked out. my excitement turned to sadness that afternoon when the utility company came to fill in my hole and beloved "dinosaur bone".

i pretended to go camping in my front yard with my red fanny pack and my mud pies.

when i was 7, i lived in a farm house that was over 100 years old. there was a barn on the property as well, and outside of the barn a giant wood framed structure that i thought was a flying saucer. i spent hours playing on that structure imagining i was flying my saucer to far off places.

i decided that i was
president of the
rainbow club

FIRSTS

FiRSTS

i had my first

           mental breakdown when i was seven.

     i will never forget it.
     walking out
               to recess one day, if
               finally dawned

    on my that
    i had my
    own internal,
    continuing,
    monologue.

      over the next few days i grew
      increasingly anxious and withdrawn

         - not being able
         to get out of my
         own head.

    this all leading up to a panic attack,

before my
parents finally
understood what
was happening
in my little
baby brain.   they scheduled me an
          appointment
               with therapist soon
               after, and so began

        a lifetime of

      anxiety
      issues
           and mental illness.

for the first time ever, i didn't do a school project and the teacher had to call my parents at home. ironically, it was for art class. i was very embarrassed.

I made my father chase a rainbow with me. I was convinced that we would find gold at the end. I remember seeing my first rainbow and rushing to put on my red canvas sneakers. He tried to explain that rainbows were an illusion but I wouldn't believe it. so I ran and ran and when I thought I was getting close the rainbow seemed to jump across the field to a distant hill. I kept running and running until I finally realized that I was never going to catch up and I just stood there disappointed but also admiring how beautiful, large and absolutely unattainable that rainbow was for me. Even now, approaching 50, I remember that feeling and I still want to cry.

went to israel for my first time

i was out snow tubing with my father at a state park with lots of other families and my dad put me on an inflatable tube and pushed me down spinning me. i spun all the way down the hill my head hanging off the side and i rotated directly into an electrical box. the first time i got stitches.

i remember my mother slapping me for drinking out of the "colored" water fountain at jcpenny..then she took me to see my first 3d movie..house of wax at the movie theater. it *1953*

i got to ride a horse for the first time by myself

when i was 7, my mom and i went to seattle to visit her friends from college. while there, i went on a ferris wheel for the first time. it was a really big one-- it gave a view of the city and the wharf. i was absolutely enchanted by it. my hands gripped the side of the box that held me and i just stared, starry-eyed, out at the view of the city. it was the most beautiful thing i'd ever seen.

FIRSTS

it was the first time i won anything. i put in a single ticket to win a bicycle at my local grocery store and i won! it the first time i had ever won anything and it was awesome. that is until i told them i wanted the black bike, not the pink one (yep, i'm a girl so i'm supposed to be born with an innate love of all things pink). i remember the look everyone gave me seemed so uncomfortable, more for them than me. i clearly recall wondering why adults were so strange... why in the world would they get upset over my decision about a color?

When I was 7 years old, I was finishing first grade at an air force base where my father was stationed. During that summer, I got my first kiss on the lips from a girl that lived next door. Several weeks later, she moved away and I never saw her again.

my aunt had a pearl necklace and earrings that was first time i ever saw a pair and she gave them both to me

i had my first 'boyfriend' at 7. he sat behind me in mr. stewart's class. we passed notes daily. it was fun and innocent. i miss those days.

my grandparents died when i was seven. that was my first death that i was old enough to understand. i stood in the vestibule of the church with my grandmother's casket telling her it was okay to come out now, we would laugh at the joke.

when i was 7 years old i went to canada for the first time. my sister was in the "canam" program where the canadians would play softball here for a weekend and then we would go up there. we stayed in a rural area quebec and got to know the locals through gestures because of the french/english language barrier. it was then that i learned that we are all more alike than different in this world. i fell in love with traveling and meeting strangers and i can't wait to meet people whom i haven't met yet.

FIRSTS

my family and i moved from california to germany for my dad's job when i was 7 years old. i remember the long flight to frankfurt, getting off the plane and touching snow for the first time. we lived in a hotel for 4 weeks until my parents found a home to rent. the hotel turned the heat off at night. my mom would use a blow dryer in the mornings to warm us up.

i was called "nigger" for the first time. i didn't know what it meant. i don't think she did either.

when i was 7 i took my first flight on an airplane, traveling from dhaka, bangladesh to los angeles, california

my grandad took me to my first ballgame when i was 7. it was a yankees game and we were on the third base line. i remember i had one of those awful, polyester graphic tees on that day. nothing beats a hotdog at the ballpark with your grandad. think i'm going to buy some tickets tonight for the two of us. i'm 43, but i'll feel like i'm 7 again.

when i was 7 years old, i got my first menorah as a hanukkah present. i still have it 22 years later.

I had my first kiss, her name was Amanda.

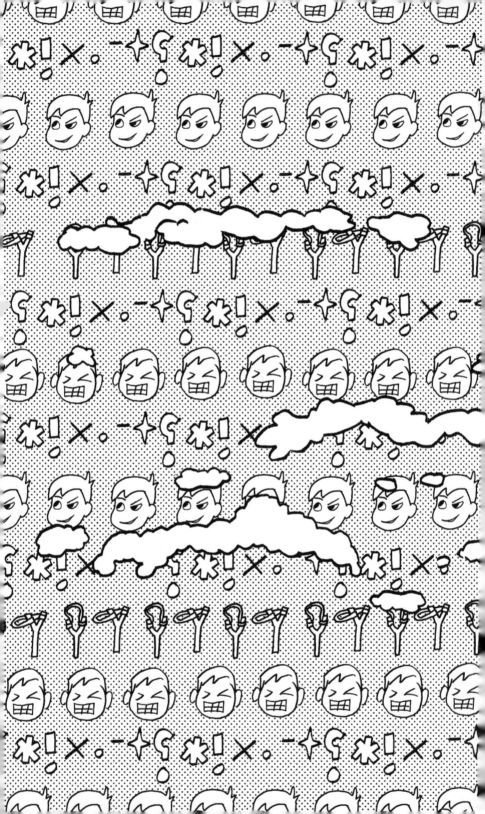

i used to blow up ant
hills with firecrackers.

MISCHIEF

sneaking muscadines from my grandfather's grape vines at his camp on the lake in louisiana

Told my parents that my teacher hit me; this was the reason I didnot attend class. It was not true

My baby brother was born when I was 7, and I was suddenly no longer the baby. I'm told that I did crazy things to act out my frustration - I colored our bathroom yellow, I squeezed an entire tube of toothpaste into the sink - I didn't want a brother, but now I love him dearly!

on my family's biggest move from connecticut down to west palm beach my father had stopped for gas and found my sister and i with our faces completely colored in with green crayola marker.

when i was seven, me and my best friend were at home by ourselves and were playing catch and accidentally broke my moms special napkin holder that had prayer hands and a bible verse. we freaked out and eventually glued it back together with gorilla glue. 18 years later you can still find that napkin holder at my house

i was a child actor in taiwan at the time. one time i was on a show with chow young fat, and i was throwing a tantrum and crying. he kneeled down and tried to comfort me..then i kicked him. it was all over the news the next day.

I realized I was the only one getting yelled at for running around without a shirt on.

194

MISCHIEF

When I was
7, I remember
my parents used
to leave me alone
while they ran short
errands. This was in 1962
so it wasn't unusual. I would
wait a few minutes and then get
into a drawer in a buffet to get
a nickel. My father had a snow
cone route and the money from
sales were put into the drawer.
When I thought the coast was
clear, I would get a nickel and
go to the corner store nearby.
There, I would buy a box of
candy cigarettes. After my
purchase, I would go
home and be back
before my parents
got home. One
time, they left my 3
year old brother with me.
I grabbed two nickels and
we went to the store to get our
candy. He slowed me down and
when we were walking home, I
saw our parent's car. I took off
running with my brother behind
me. We were running up the
walkway from the sidewalk to the
porch when my brother fell down.
He knocked out his two front
teeth and was unconscious. I
was scared and relieved
because it delayed my
getting in trouble.

MISCHIEF

when i
was seven i
enjoyed riding
a bike around the
cul-de-sac with my
friends. these girls were
my everyday playmates
as we were neighbors and
we played outside at every
opportunity. a new boy
our age moved in around
the corner from us and
for whatever reason, his
presence set us girls on
edge and we decided we
didn't want him playing with
us. we discussed what
to do and i told them
to leave it to me.
i had been
watching my
brothers earlier
throwing dirt clods
at each other, so i went
and gathered a big pocketful
of them. when the new boy
approached, i summoned him
over and proceeded to stuff
his tube socks with dirt clods
and then smack them to
break them inside his socks.
he left crying. watching him
walk away crying struck
me so deeply that the
memory can still
draw a tear from
me. 🥶

196

CUSSING

my sister caught me calling her a "bitch" because she was taking forever in the restroom and i was too lazy to go to the one downstairs. never did that again...

when i was 7 i cussed out my grandma

MISCHIEF

Well, we were living in Georgia at the time, the neighbor kid across the street (a boy) would always call me madame putting emphasis on the word "damn". I asked him nicely to please not call me that . Of course he replied, but why Ma"damn" I am only addressing you . I said no, call me Beth. He said, ok, ma "damn" Beth. I said, "If you call me ma"d%$#" again, I will beat you up. He said, "really, Ma'damn" I would like to see you try. Needless to say, (with me having 2 older brothers), I could back up what I said, so I blackened his eye and busted his lip. So, what do you think he called me after that...? Badass Beth, ugh...here we go again...

When
I was
7, I was
beginning
to learn about
cuss words. When
no one was watching,
I'd go into the bedroom
corner and say a cuss word.

PRANK

at 7 i used to make mud pies. i convinced a neighbor boy the mud pie was a brownie and he ate it.

7 years old memory: i got mad at my parents and i took my brothers compass from his math class and poked tons of holes in their water bed, under their pillows. they didnt realize until they went to bed. no one slept well that night.

when i was 7 years old i convinced all of my friends that baby spice from the spice girls was my mom.

my mom and i were living with her friend kevin. he had a two floor house with a drum set set up in the basement. one day i decided to wrap the whole set in toilet paper, resulting is using about 4-5 full rolls of tp. my mom was the first to find it and was so pissed at me. i had to rewrap every roll i used. i don't think kevin ever found out.

MISCHIEF

joe latona pulled the dish mat out from underneath mrs. mcglory feet causing her to fall on top of him.

i remember playing transformers with the other kids. i was always hawk woman because she was the only cool girl transformer. this was when the show was a cgi animation and all the characters were animals rather than trucks or cars. i also remember putting a red ant in a kid's shoe as a prank and the ant bit me and i had to go to the nurses office. karma

i was the youngest in my family by over 4 years; an older sister and two older half-brothers. when my brothers visited over the summer, i was often left out. but one year i finally got to be in on the fun. you know how sometimes when you move your eyes fast from focusing on one thing to focus on another you get this white ghostly flash in your peripheral vision? well my siblings had convinced the younger brother that it was actually a being. a ghostly, but real, life form. so we went "hunting" one day while he was away. concocted an elaborate story of how we killed the creature as it tried to attack a friend. we got that friend in on the story, carved a mop handle to a point, colored it and slathered it in fake "blood", ruffled our hair, muddied our shoes... we played it up big time. he swears he didn't believe us but he also insisted he didn't want to sleep alone that night. to this day i'm still not sure if anyone told him the real story.

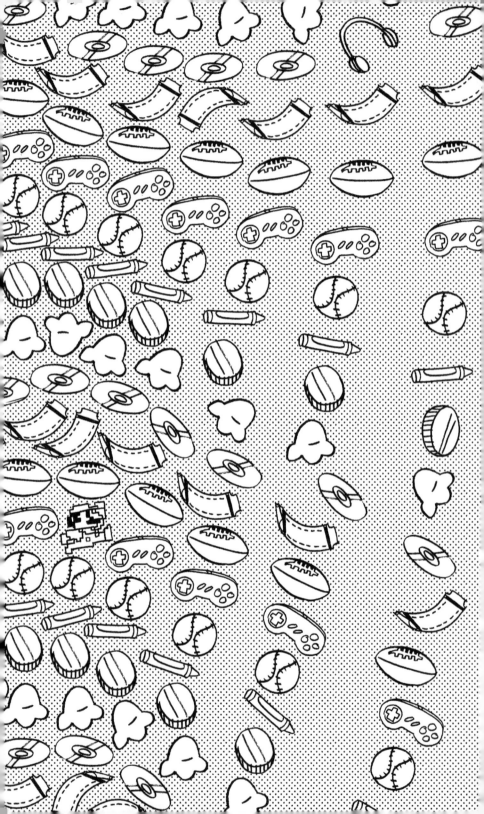

ENTERTAINMENT

ENTERTAINMENT

I was an avid reader at 7, pouring over any book I could get my hands on. As a Birthday present my Aunt gave me Oliver Twist. She was equally as excited for me to start reading so we curled up on the couch together, reading it aloud. From then on we made dates to sit on my Memaw's couch reading Oliver Twist until it was finished.

When I was 7... I joined the circus which was one of the best experiences of my life

in 1987, there was nothing more important on earth than the nintendo entertainment system. mario. tetris. zelda. metroid. my brother and i argued constantly and fiercely, but when the current issue of nintendo power magazine hit the mailbox we were instantly united in the common goal of defeating the next boss, advancing to the next level, or unlocking hidden treasure. up, up, down, down, left, right, left, right, b, a, start

i did a tap dance on the bozo the clown show in michigan.

i can remember learning how to whistle and being amazed that i could finally do it

ENTERTAINMENT

i can faintly remember my brother coming out of the shower in his towel, only to go in the room where my dad was, listening to led zeppelin. they had a discussion about the song being played. and i liked the song. i walked into the living room and sat in front of a shelf full of my dad's cd's, mostly rock. i picked up an album and went through the little booklet in the front and found the lyrics to "stairway to heaven", the song that was playing. reading the lyrics, nothing made sense to me. i do remember asking my brother about the song. he said i was too young to understand. it wasn't that i was too young to experience it, because i loved the song and still get that same feeling, it's just that as i got older, the song grew a different meaning to me, and it still does. and it will continue to. that songs holds a special place in my heart. and i start to understand the lyrics more and more. i was only 7

i read my first book. "mr. grump." it included through provoking lines like, "mr. grump, mr. grump, mr. grump grump grump." i still vividly remember it twenty years later.

i was sitting in the car with my dad. he handed me 2 8 track tapes. one was the popeye soundtrack and one was yes fragile. he td me to show mom the popeye one but to keep the yes tape to myself. this is the first time i ever heard rock like this and it touched me so much i fell in love with music forever. this was the last memory of dad as he passed away shortly after. to this day that album remains my favorite and music moves every aspect of my life.

my 7-year-old memories include a black beanbag. it was so big my entire body was sucked inside when i sat in it to watch my cartoons after school. i loved watching the popples & rainbow brite. i'd grab my stuffed animals, jump in the beanbag & watch my shows.

ENTERTAINMENT

i remember almost causing
my parents to have a heart
attack. it was late at night
for seven year old me,
probably about eight o'clock.
i remembered seeing a
picture that looked like
greek writing in a dictionary.
at the time, my sister was
reading percy jackson and
i really wanted to read it. i
couldn't fall asleep because
the writing in the dictionary
(which turned out to just be a
few stick figures and poorly
drawn trees doodled in) was
calling to me. it might lead
me to percy jackson! i snuck
out of bed, turned on the
night light under my desk,
and began to flip through the
dictionary. cue my parents
walking in to my room to
make sure i'm safely asleep.
i curled up smaller into the
nook under my desk so that
they didn't see me. my mom
said something in a whisper
to my dad, and he went
running through the house.
i was hidden for so long my
parents almost called the
police. i came out right before
they did, and they were so
relieved they forgot to punish
me. this was about the
time that i realized i was an
english and novel geek.

one of my memories from when i was seven was going to a pumpkin launching festival with my parents.

at 7 yrs old i was still doing modeling. while i have great memories now (even being in italian vogue kid edition). but i remember absolutly hating going on auditions. one in particular was sitting in the last interview with i believe producers from mr. belvedere. he asked how much i enjoy doing this and i blurted out how much i hated it. needless to say the part of wesley went elsewhere.

🎶 playful obsession with the us arrival of the beatles! 🎶

i don't remember many things from my childhood, but the summer of 1982 i remember the song "hold me" by fleetwood mac. i was at the swimming pool and it was playing on the loudspeaker. for whatever reason- i remember i was happy and actually enjoying myself. i flash back to that precise moment when i hear that song again.

my parents told me we were going to visit their friends, the bbs. they ended up surprising me and taking me to a beach boys concert.

ART

almost knocking over a
famous painting at met art
museum in ny

when i was 7 years old
my first piece of artwork
was featured in a fine arts
festival at my school. since
then, i've grown as an
artist and now my artwork
is found in several art
shows. from being 7 years
old, i have found a sense
of pride in my works.

going to visit my grandfather and he would paint in his studio. i would lay on the floor with crayons and color, he would paint and listen to mozart.

When I was 7, I made a turtle out of newspaper and paper mache for art class. I painted him green. He was ugly but I loved him. So did my Mom.

around thanksgiving, my 1st grade teacher (1979) told me i was coloring my picture of my indian girl "wrong".. it was for a collage display and everyone in class was coloring a piece of it.. pilgrims, cornucopia, food, etc... i was using vertical zigzags to show the weave of her clothes. i planned on the same for the feathers in her hair. we went back and forth a bit about it, and i knew then that i was an artist because i stood fast with my vision even if she disagreed!

When I was 7 years old I thought I could be a Artist

when i was 7 i started my first art scrapbook and drew sketches of clothes to practice becoming a fashion designer.

1969, one of my most vivid memories is looking at my peter max poster tacked to the wall of my bedroom. i was in love with the colors. who knew 40 years later i'd meet the man and now have a signed peter max...still next to my bed.

i remember being really excited about a pelican drawing i did. i've been drawing since i was that young and quite honestly that pelican is still one of my favorites. i remember that pelican more than i remember anything else. i always like to joke that it's my best work. and since it has had such a lasting effect 20 years later, i guess it actually is!

MOVIES

when i was 7 years old i saw one of my favorite movies, xanadu. i became obsessed. i got the soundtrack on cassette tape and spent many hours roller skating to it in my backyard. when it came out on hbo i watched it every chance i had. i still love listening to the soundtrack. great memories for me!

star wars!!!

In 1966, my parents took me to the cinema to watch "Born Free", a movie which has inspired me ever since. A heart-warming, amazing film on the incredible liaison between the lioness Elsa and the people who raised her in Kenya, Joy and George Adamson. From this beautiful real life story I have learned about empathy and connection with animals. A wonderful memory!

ENTERTAINMENT

when i was 7, mrs. doubtfire was in the theaters. i remember going to see it with my mother and aunt. they let me sit a row in front of them, and bought me those butterfinger pieces. it was the first film i remember seeing in a theater, and it started a life-long admiration for robin williams.

i was in second grade when my class and some higher grades were gathered to watch the *70s* love-fest 'free to be you and me'. when the film showed rosey grier singing "it's all right to cry," all the older kids started giggling and catcalling me, because i was a crier, and everyone knew it wasn't okay for boys to cry. i was teased and smacked around for weeks after we watched that movie, each of my tormentors telling me to cry because rosey grier said it was "all right."

going to see planet of the apes at the drive- in movie theatre!

when i was 7 years old, my mother, sister, brother, and i lived with some friends in a big old farm house out in the boonies, in a tiny town called freedom, maine. our closest neighbors lived about a mile up the dirt road, and to my young mind, they were wicked rich. we didn't go over very often, but when we did, they'd let us watch movies on their laser disc player. the only kid-friendly movies they had were the apple dumpling gang, the sound of music, and tron. i still love all of these movies, though i've never again had the opportunity to watch them on laser disc!

i went to see star wars when it first came out in theaters.

i remember my teacher setting up a movie day for the entirety of the second grade. the movie was old yeller. i will never understand why she choose this movie, but there wasn't a dry eye in sight and plenty of traumatized students left school that day.

i saw the movie
big and wanted to
be josh baskin.

ENTERTAINMENT

oh boy, that's a long while ago and i can only really recall one small story. when i was 7 years old in **1995**, i remember seeing a trailer for a movie that gave me a feeling that sticks with me to this day. the trailer was for dr. jekyll and ms. hyde. a comedy about a man who drinks a concotion that turns him into a power hungry woman. seeing that trailer is the very first memory i can recall of wishing that could happen to me. it's the first piece of

watching back to the future

when i was 7 there was a pg 13 movie my brother wanted to see, my aunt pretended to see if we could sneak into the theater just to see the cool new seats with cup holders, and when we got in she said let's stay. i thought we got away with sneaking in, but really she just bought us tickets!

When I was seven, I went to go see the original Star Wars at the movies. It was awesome! I dreamed of traveling to other planets like Luke, having a mentor like Yoda, and robots for friends. Seven was a good a good year!

NEWS

here is an indelible memory from age 7: i was in first grade. around noon one day they closed the entire school and sent us all home. when i got home my parents were also home from work and my mother was crying. the tv was on and on the news they reported that president john f. kennedy had been shot in dallas and killed.

i didn't really understand 9/11. honestly i was just very excited to get to leave school early.

i knit a red, white, and blue scarf for richard nixon while he was campaigning for president in 1972.

a memory from when i was seven years old: images from news television during the gulf war: the green flashes of lights that filled up the night skies of iraq are the first images of war i ever witnessed. in my elementary school music class around the same time, we were obligated to sing patriotic songs and in english class we were obligated to write pen pal letters to soldiers in the midst of violence. all of this seemed incongruous.

the death of kurt cobain being covered by the media

when i was 7 years old
it was the year 9/11
happened. i'll never forget
coming home from school
in winona, minnesota
and seeing my mom
glued to the tv. i couldn't
fully comprehend what
was happening, but it's
something that will stick
with me forever.

ENTERTAINMENT

SPORTS

on my 7th birthday, it was opening day of little league. it was the year 1959, and mickey mantle was my idol. there was an opening day parade, i wore #7, and i was so excited that i completely forgot that it was my birthday. my team was the tigers (not the yankees) and i played 2nd base (not center field) but i still thought i'd be like mick!

my dad dug out a flat area in our backyard and had a large concrete pad installed. we then dug a hole for a basketball pole. the pole was formed and welded together by my grandpa who worked as a welder for the local steel company. i ended up playing hours and hours of basketball on the court

i missed the olympics
that year. the soviet union
boycotted the games
and there was no official
coverage of the event.

i remember playing little
league for the first time
at age 7. i was the kid
kicking dandelions in the
outfield. i line drive cane
flying at me and managed
to hit me in the front of my
left ankle. it hurt. i didn't
realize i had been cut until
i took my cleats off and
my sock was covered in
blood. i remember the fear
because i had never seen
that much blood come out
of me before. although i
finished the season, that
was my only year playing
baseball.

at age 7, my brother
and i played basketball
with a tennis ball on the
sidewalk. we counted off
a set number of concrete
squares, and used the
squares on each end as
baskets.

i remember finding four
leaf clovers and having my
mom dye my hair green for
little league.

a youth football program
was handing out flyers
to our 2nd grade class.
i was so excited at the
thought of playing football.
i was very shy, but i was
also the strong & tough
kid among my friends. at
lunch, my friend went with
me to the table to get a
football flyer. they handed
us cheerleading ones,
and told us that girls don't
do football. i was silently
livid, and threw the flyer
in the garbage can next
to the table and walked
away. i wish i'd been more
outspoken at the time to
challenge that idea and just
play anyways. i wasn't, but
now i teach my younger
siblings that they can be.

getting waked up in the
afternoon and getting to
go see my brother play in
his basketball game and
getting really happy bc he
made a buzzer beater

first year of playing little
league baseball. love
baseball still.

ENTERTAINMENT

Going to a Falcons vs Saints football game with my dad

i entered, and won, a contest to go out on the ice with one of the la kings. autographed hockey stick, my own jersey, seats directly behind the glass... but they left out the locker room tour, though, because i was a little girl. i still have the jersey, stick, and picture, almost 30 years later.

i remember taking a summer long gymnastics course while staying with my nanny and papa in twenty-nine palms. when i was done and came back to orange county i met peter vidmar (an olympic gold medalist). he asked me to show him some stuff. he liked what he saw and encouraged my mom to take me to scats to train because he believed i had what it takes to earn myself some medals one day but unfortunately we couldn't afford it.

i went to my first baseball game at 7. i was excited about pizza and ice cream. i was sure that the cleveland indians were the best team of all time. as i grew up i realized just how special mid 90's cleveland baseball was. it sparked my love for the team and ihe city of cleveland. i've spent years since researching the history of the team and the city.

CAR

CAR

my dad had just been stationed in arizona. there was a little wash in the road as you entered our little post subdivision. back then, we would ride in the back of the pickup truck, in the bed, unrestrained. if it had rained, dad would drive through the wash kind of fast to make the water splash up. and the water drops that landed on our hands were called "wishes". we got one wish for every drop.

i was 7 years old and my brother was almost 5 years old our mom was a single mom , but a hard worker she worked as a dietician at unity hospital, but we didnt have much money, i remember the summer before going into 3rd grade we got in our moms little red dodge dart, no air conditioning(windows down), and she drove us to taylor falls for 2 days we slept in the car ate chips, peanut butter sandwiches, but it was awesome!!!!... what a beautiful sight and fun memories!!!

my mom took me and my twin brother to visit san francisco. we drove from salt lake city with my dad's cousin and her family. there were six of us in one vw rabbit! we left early in the morning while it was still dark. i watched out the window and saw my first shooting star.

i vividly remember riding in a limo with my mom and big sister. there was a fridge stocked with soda. i was allowed to take a pepsi and drink it all!! we were on our way to jfk. i remember looking at the city approaching new york. it was huge. tall buildings. bright lights. big bridges. we were leaving our life in new jersey and moving to ireland. my mom was diagnosed with breast cancer and my father left. she was an immigrant and when he left she wanted to move back to ireland. i had no idea that getting into that limo was going to change my life forever but i am glad i did!

CAR

in the second grade, our class exchanged gifts at christmas. i always looked forward to gift exchanges, because i am thrilled with the concept of getting a gift that had the potential of being a thing never before in my consciousness. we put the gifts in a pile and numbered them. each child drew a number and enjoyed the thrill of opening something new and surprising. that year, i got an interesting surprise. the gift i drew was wrapped in tattered paper. clearly, it was wrapped by another 7 year old. when i opened it, i found a toy car that had been run over by an actual car. there was dirt smashed into the toy. i retreated to my seat and hid what was once a new toy car, but was now a beaten up mess. other kids were showing off their new toys, but i couldn't bring myself to show mine. later, another boy came to me and asked, "do you like your car. i saw you got my gift, it was my favorite before i gave it away." after that, i realized that i was given a gift that was all another kid had to give. solid!

CAR

in **1964** when i was 7 years old, a man in his car stopped me on my way home from school and exposed himself to me. i ran home and told my mother and she told me to take a different way home. not too long after that on my new route home, i recognized his car from several blocks away and ran into an overgrown field by the road. his car came to a skidding halt about 20 feet from where i was laying throwing gravel and dirt into the air. i laid on my stomach as still as a stone and watched his eyes in the rear view mirror while swirls of dust settled around his car--thinking--he doesn't see me. he doesn't see me. he doesn't see me. then he drove away.

the thing i remember most vividly was my dad explaining to me that my mom was almost involved in a car accident. she had multiple sclerosis and the shock from the near miss triggered it into full swing and she became paralyzed from the neck down.

when i was 7 i went on a short road trip with my grandparents from fargo, where they lived, back to my home in st. cloud. we were driving back in my grandfathers very large brown-olive colored impala, and driving just under the speed limit. the seats were bench seats and after we stopped to eat in fergus falls my grandma let me climb into the front sit between them. we kept track of where all the license plates were from. mostly mn and nd, which should have been boring. but i remember that trip as fun! probably because my grandma was my favorite person in the world.

CAR

i remember standing on the transmission housing "hump" in the back seat of my mom's *1972* chevy nova while she waited her turn in line for gas during the oil crisis. her licence number, ddp 285 (yup...i remember that!), meant that she could only buy gas on odd days, because her plate number was odd.

WHEN I WAS 7, I THOUGHT THE WORD "CHEVROLET" WAS JUST ABOUT THE COOLEST WORD, BUT INSISTED YOU PRONOUNCED CHEVROLET WITH A HARD "LET" AT THE END. I STOOD UP IN FRONT OF MY SECOND GRADE CLASS AND TOTALLY FIBBED ABOUT MY FATHER GOING TO PARIS ON A BUSINESS TRIP - HE WAS A VETERINARIAN. IT'S ALSO THE YEAR I LEARNED ABOUT DIVORCE FROM MY FRIEND WHOSE PARENTS "DID NOT LOVE EACH OTHER ANY MORE".

CAR

when i was 7 years
old me and my sister
ran my brother over
in a barbie jeep.

CAR

when i was seven years old i decided to start going to church, primarily because they came to pick me up in a big orange bus. i felt deprived because i assumed all children took a school bus to school, but we lived a block away from my school and i had to walk each day. of course, this was prior to my exposure to riding a greyhound bus, which would tarnish my love affair with big busses. but that was still a few years away.

my parents were divorced and i would travel between iowa and alabama to visit them. some of the best memories i have are riding in the car and staring out at the stars and the clouds during the long trips.

i hustled the neighborhood kids for money to ride in my moms car while she was on bed rest after her hysterectomy.

i remember when i was 7 at the end of every summer me and my brother would wait around in front of our apartment waiting for ups truck hoping he would bring us a package full of goodies from our grandparents and when we did get it me and my brother would actually work together for once to bring it upstairs for our mom to open it for us

when i was 7, i remember riding in the backseat of my mom's car as she would take my brother and i with her on her errands. i loved looking out the window at the world. i loved the possibility that we could go anywhere the car could take us.

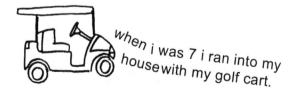

when i was 7 i ran into my house with my golf cart.

226

FULL CIRCLE

FULL CIRCLE

when i was 7 years old i met the man i have now been with for 5 years.

i was about 7 years old when i got my first camera as a gift. it was **1969**, and i was given a cheap, plastic point-and-shoot film camera for a vacation up to the snow. i took horrible pictures with it; everyone was cut off and the lighting was washed out. even though my photos were bad, i was hooked on cameras from that point on. i'm now a middle school photography teacher.

When I was seven me and my best friend tried to steal some plums from our next door neighbours plum tree. We were already afraid of him, since he was old, and a bit grumpy. He caught us and started yelling (as I remember it), we got so scared we ran, ran, ran. Later that day he showed up with a bowl of plums at both our parents houses. I think he was actually quite nice.

FULL CIRCLE

when i was seven years old i was a quiet kid, but there were several of who bullied this one boy. i remember one day in particular that we punched him and pushed him down. it was like lord of the flies. it's an aweful memory and as i see his son as a senior at the high school where i teach i am constantly reminded of the darkest part of my young persona.

i was in mrs. southwards class. she called for the line leaders to line up. nobody lined up. i decided to be snarky and ask for "living leeeeaders". the look she gave me for my sass was enough to make me silent for the rest of the year. 35 years later and i am now the teacher in that very same classroom.

when i was 7 years old i held a camera for the first time. i still remember how powerful i felt with it in my hands that one moment changed my life. i now am a videographer and film maker. if i never picked up the camera i never would have started to like cameras which brought me to where i am today

When I was 7 years old, my English was horrible and I was so afraid to speak in class because others would make fun of me. But my first grade teacher, Ms. Thomas, never made me feel bad for messing up. She would always greet me with a warm smile and a hug each day; she gave me books to read, made us sing songs, and showered me with love. I started reading anything I could get a hold of. I would stay after school with Ms. Thomas and she made me feel safe. She made a difference in who I am today and now in memory of her and many teachers/mentors, I am now a teacher too.

Behind this book-

Hi, Phil here. As we all have heard there's a mind boggling horrible war in Syria happening right now. For a lot of people (myself included), war on the other side of the world is hard to relate to. But there was one story in the Syrian war that captured my attention and millions of other people around the world. Directly in the middle of this war and humanitarian crisis is a town called Aleppo. In that town was a 7 year old girl named Bana Alabed. She lived with her family and would live tweet the death and destruction as it happened around her. It was horrifying.

I am someone that processes life through talking and stories. So I began thinking about what I was doing at the age of 7, asking other people their memories, and trying to understand war from that perspective. I couldn't, it's not understandable. Yet this experience of asking my loved ones about memories from when they were 7 was moving.

I am also someone that processes life through art, in this case, trying to understand war. Bringing the stories I had heard into my art was a natural step. Opening it up further to hear memories from anyone pushed the project even further. In the end, what was created, was a portrait of Bana Alabed standing amongst the rubble of her neighborhood. This portrait measures 24 feet wide, 12 and a half feet tall, and was created by handwriting the hundreds of stories found in this book. I find it haunting.

When people shared memories they had no idea what image those words would help create. This was intentional as it helped people share a memory free of the pressure that might come with knowing where their story would go. The decision has also been made to not include the artwork in this book. Reading, hearing, and sharing people's stories always felt like an experience unto itself, keeping them separate for you to read here just feels right. But if you'd like to see the art please head over to philinthecircle.com.

CPSIA information can be obtained
at www.ICGtesting.com
Printed in the USA
BVHW06s0451170418
513497BV00005B/36/P

9 780692 076750